AMAZING STORIES FROM THE STREETS

Dr Charles J Margerison

Published by
Amazing People Publications Ltd.
10 Grange Road, West Kirby,
Wirral, Merseyside, England C48 4HA
Email: frances@amazingpeopleworldwide.com
Web: www.amazingpeopleworldwide.com & www.amazingpeopleinstitute.com

Disclaimer

These published materials represent the views of the author. The stories reflect the experiences of people's lives in general, and do not relate to any specific person. They are interpretations made by the author, based on his own ideas and thoughts. The interpretations are made in good faith, recognising that other interpretations could be made. The author and publisher disclaim any responsibility from action that readers take on the stories, for educational or other purposes. Any use of these materials is the responsibility of the reader.

Print ISBN 978-1-9163727-0-2

CONTENTS

Introduction

At the end of each day, as we fall asleep, we can reflect on the places to which we have been. As I have travelled the world, visiting many countries and seeing people from different cultures, I have tried to capture the main ideas from the people I have met, in a collection of short stories.

I call these, *Amazing Stories From The Streets.* They are images and insights that I have gained from walking through many streets, from the dusty, unmade roads of Costa Rica through to the palatial avenues of Paris. In between, I have had the opportunity to meet with people from different walks of life: poor people in South Africa and corporate executives from the USA and Europe. All of them had a story to tell, but rarely was it shared beyond the confines of family and friends.

In this book, I have captured my impressions of the characters and the culture of people from Australia, Argentina, Italy, Poland, Spain and many other countries. The stories are told in a similar way to that developed by Jacques Prevert, a great French poet of the streets, and also Walt Whitman, the American author. I have used my training as a psychologist to interpret meetings and events on my road of life. I have also imagined conversations with characters from history who can share their lessons in life.

You will meet Wanted Man, The Priest, The Refugee, Silent Children, The Messenger, The Coffee Pickers, The Lady in Black, and many more. Their stories may influence your life and what you do with your time.

These stories may inspire you to record your impressions of what you see and hear. As a result, you can develop your skills of thinking and writing. Most importantly, you can improve your self-confidence in expressing what you feel about the people you meet on your streets of life. In doing so, you can learn more about yourself and how to make the best of your opportunities.
To that end, I have developed the term *Conversology*, which is the way we can study and improve our discussions. I hope these stories will facilitate useful conversations to help you learn more about your own lives.

Character education is now seen as a vital aspect of student and adult development for life. These stories, derived from real life, provide an easy way to consider the issues and implications. To facilitate this, I have provided some questions for discussion and project work.

Dr Charles Margerison.
December 2019

Introduction

AMAZING STORIES FROM THE STREETS

STREETS OF WAR

Throughout the ages, fear has engulfed villages, towns and cities, as invaders attack. That happened to me. I was born in England during 1940, as bombs from German planes rained down around my parents' home. Lives were devastated.

I have, therefore, tried to capture thoughts of those caught in the crossfire of conflict. To do so, I have walked battle lines and streets of war, from the Roman invasions to modern day. I have written short stories to reflect my perceptions of unrecognised heroes and heroines. Millions of people never had the chance to write their own story. I am one of the fortunate ones.

Devastation

Overview

At the start of World War II, the Germans tried to bomb Britain into submission. After London, their main target was Birkenhead and Liverpool, where the deep water docks enabled ships to bring in food and munitions.

I was born near those docks, just three days after the bombing commenced. These are some of my memories.

Rubble in the streets.
Yesterday, they were our houses and are now ruins.
People who had a home, now homeless.
The bombers have wrought havoc.
Another night of destruction and devastation.
The Germans unleashing death from the skies,
Murdering randomly,
Trying to kill my family and me,
Trying to kill and maim other families,
Merseyside, and the ports, their target,
Liverpool and Birkenhead, the major cities.
A couple of miles away, I was born

September 1940.
The start of what became known as 'The Blitz.'
Night after night of bombs and incendiaries.
35,000 tons of bombs.
My mother took me to the caves,
Quarries dug into the hills.
There, with her sisters, we hid under the earth.
The caves were our only protection.
Yet, the rats found us:
Real big ones
Just as frightening as the German bombs.
Endless nights waiting for daylight.
Would we see another day?
What food would we have?
Sadly, many who did not have the caves died.
No protection, no mercy, no chance.
'The Blitz' they called it.
Nazi bombers unleashing death
Then flying home to a warm breakfast,
No doubt joking about a good night's work,
Leaving the Merseysiders to bury their dead.
Fathers, Mothers, Sons and Daughters,
Aunts, Uncles, Nieces and Nephews,
Friends and Neighbours,
No one was spared.
But my mother in the caves, despite the rats, saved me.

Questions

Is bombing ever justified and, if so, under what conditions?

What can you do to prepare for attacks in your life, which can negatively impact your career and family situations?

Last Man

Overview

As with all wars, there are people who survive, but their life is ruined. They carry the trauma of their experiences, whether they are physical injuries or mental health issues. In many cases, they have lost family and friends.

This was a common occurrence for many soldiers during and after the 1st and 2nd World Wars.

This story was inspired by reading the work of Jacques Prevert, the great French writer, whose book, *Les Paroles*, provided a framework for me to develop a style of writing that I call 'prosoems', which is a mix of prose and poem.

His hair is grey, his face wrinkled.
Sipping his tea, he reflects on his life.
The good times, the bad times,
The sunny days, the freezing days.
Remembering his youth:
Little food or water,
A continual ache in his stomach.
Then the call to war in 1914.
Running between the trenches,
The unforgettable horror.
Thunder in the sky.
Mud and blood on the ground.

Fighting the Germans.
Surviving against the odds.
Shell shocked, eardrums burst.
Gas, delirium.
But alive!
Returning home
To a town that no longer existed,
Parents killed by the Germans.
'Brothers and sisters also dead,' said the girl next door.
He cared for her.
They marry and have three children.
He works as a labourer to rebuild the town.
Hard work, in all weather.
Until the call again, in 1939, to defend France.
The Germans, once more, ravaging and raping.
Five years of war, but he survives yet again.
Now, he sits in the town square
Too old to run, to work or to fight.
No one with whom to talk, as he sips his tea.
His colleagues in war have gone.
His wife is dead.
Passers-by see only an old man in a grey coat.
He watches in silence.
Who wants to talk about the past?
France lives because of him and his generation.
The Last Man.

Questions

Within your own life, who do you feel most closely resembles the 'last man' described in this story?

Would you stop and speak with him, and what would you say?

Mates

Overview

This story is also called 'The Last Conversation.' It suggests the words which may have been spoken between two English soldiers who had developed a friendship whilst in the battlefield.

The dialogue is broken up, using normal and italic text, to identify the lines spoken by each soldier.

Just a few more days and it should all be over.
That's what they said four years ago, and the war still rolls on.

Yes, but you can see the Germans are retreating.
They have regrouped before, like they did on the Somme in 1916.

I think it is different now they know the Yanks are fighting.
But, Uncle Sam's lads will not help us in this Belgian village.
I hope they do and bring new weapons and chewing gum.
The USA guys will be sent to liberate Paris and Brussels.

Yes, they will get the glory, after we have done the hard slog.
The Germans won't give up here without one last fight.

Streets Of War

We can beat them in a fair fight, if they don't use mustard gas.
They'll use anything to win.

Can't understand what they are fighting for.
Yes, who wants to live in Belgium?

What are we doing here anyway?
We are supposed to stop the Krauts getting to England.

The English Channel will do that, as they can't swim across.
Yes, our Navy is the best in the world.

Exactly, they can't invade our country!
So, what are we doing lying in this rain-sodden field?

Getting paid by His Majesty for defending the Frogs and Belgians.
If the Belgians and French could fight, we could go home.

Wish it would warm up.
No chance, it is the 3rd of November.

Looking at those clouds, we are more likely to get snow.
Do you think we will get home for Christmas?

No, I think the top brass have forgotten we are here.
Yes, it's just a bloody big chess game to them.

We are just pawns in the game.
I would like a game of football, if we get home.

At least you know what the rules are and there is a referee.
Out here, there are no rules, except that it is them or us.

It's a bit quiet.
Not sure, did you see a movement in the trees over there.
Think it is only the wind.
No, it's the Hun, watch out!

I can't, they've got me in the chest.
And me too........ All the best mate.

Questions

Who are your most important mates?

For what reasons have you chosen them?

Name On A Cross

Overview

On my various travels to France, I have visited the cemeteries where many British and Commonwealth soldiers, sailors and airmen, who were killed in the two World Wars, have been buried.

This account is about one of the days that I visited, to pay my respects to those who fought to give us all a better life.

It is the first name that I see:

Private H Shelbourne, 04982029
Age 20
The Hampshire Regiment
6th June 1944

He probably knew that he would not see the end of that day.
He was one of 133,000 who were killed at the D-Day Landings.
His name now inscribed on a simple white cross.

It is now a Saturday afternoon, 8th June 2002.
The wind and rain have soaked his grave.
Dark clouds roll above.
He would have been 78 years of age.
Probably married, and a father and a grandfather.
And what would he have done with his life?
He would have found the cure for cancer.
Maybe a great musician, or an architect, or a doctor saving lives.
Maybe he would have written a beautiful book to rival Shakespeare.
Maybe he would have sung like Caruso, or made people laugh.
Perhaps an innovator who would rival Edison,
Or a poet, like Wordsworth.
An engineer, like Brunel, or a great politician.
Probably a family man living quietly, doing good works.
But we will never know, for that day his dreams died with him,
So too the dreams of his mother and father.
Their worst fears realised, and no words can bring him back.
He, like Jesus, gave his life so that others might live.
But, why was it necessary?
After the First World War, the war to end all wars,
Why did they let Germans kill again?
There are no excuses and pathetically inadequate answers.
They died because the French could not defend their own land.
They died because Germans killed them.
Boys barely out of their teens died because politicians failed.
And what can I say to Private H Shelbourne and his mates?
That I visited and paid my respects in some small way.
I appreciate what you have done for me, my family and generation.
Rest in peace, you did your best, and you are remembered.

Question

In what ways should we continue to remember those who fought for our freedom and way of life?

Pray For Peace

Overview

War has devastated most countries, at one time or another. Today, the media conveys the sheer brutality, loss of life, and destruction that war imposes on the people and countries it visits. This story reflects the images of those caught in the crossfire.

See them huddled in the corner.
Hear the thunder of the gun.
Feel the fear of rising panic
When there's nowhere to run.

See their cottages in ruins.
Hear the cries of those in pain.
Feel the heat of icy anger
As they fight against the flames.

Pray for peace.
Pray for all.
Pray to the Almighty
Before they fall.

See the bullet holes of terror.
Hear the lightning of the night.
Feel the strength of their resistance
As they fight for their rights.

Pray for peace.
Pray for all.
Pray to the Almighty.
You make the call.

Question

Do you pray and, if so, for what?

Three Days After

Overview

All wars bring forth tales of horror. The First World War showed how barbarity could quickly overtake civilisation. To gain a better understanding, I visited many of the war fields in France, around the town of Ypres, and village of Passchendaele, in Belgium. After visiting the war fields, I wrote this story.

It had to finish sometime:
The lightning of the guns.
The deafening noise of the mortars,
The devastation of the villages,
The death and destruction.
Eventually there would be no one left.
No money to make bombs.
No one to give orders.
No one to do their bidding.
I prayed for that day.
It arrived on the 11ᵗʰ November 1918.
The 11th hour of the 11ᵗʰ day.
I had survived.

But I realised it was also my 11th hour.
My injuries were severe,
A victim of one of the last attacks.
There were no wonder medicines to fight infection.
Only time and prayer.
I celebrated, as best I could
In the field hospital with the other victims.
We had done our duty.
We had won the fight for freedom.
But at personal loss.
Many of my mates died in the war.
Some, like me, when the guns stopped firing.
For, we were all victims.

Questions

How should we commemorate the fallen?

What can be done to stop further wars?

Too Young To Live

Overview

We all make decisions that we later regret. Fortunately, some we can recover from, while other wrong judgments can lead to a chain reaction, resulting in disaster.

This story is a sad example, based on a visit I made to the cemeteries where soldiers from the 1st World War are buried.

I lied and said I was eighteen.
The sergeant didn't ask any other questions.
My mate and I went for the medical and passed easily.
We were the fittest players in our football club.
'Six weeks basic training,' said the sergeant.
Then, we could join the regiment.
It sounded better than hanging round the street corners.
No work, no money, and nothing to do.
We'd at least get three meals a day and pay.
I looked forward to getting my army uniform.
That would get the attention of the local girls.
The war would soon be over, they said.
I enjoyed the six weeks training, but not my mate.

He was 16, just out of school, and too young for the tough course.
Then, the sergeant said we were ready, but it did not feel like it.
Putting a bayonet into a real person was different than a training dummy.
We had learned to dig trenches and shoot.
Plus, all the polishing of shoes, marching and saluting.
My mate was seasick on the boat to France.
But, all seemed calm on the other side.
After living rough, we arrived in a place called Albert.
'Good name that,' said my mate, 'my dad's name is Albert.'
The blokes we met didn't think it was good place.
'Hell on Earth,' they said, 'and get prepared to kill or be killed.'
First day in the trenches was a nightmare.
Shells, bullets and blood, with guys dying all around us.
Then, the Germans attacked, but our lads just held them off.
That night my mate cried and said he could not continue.
'I'm going home,' he said, and asked me to go with him.
We had only gone four miles when they caught us.
Said we had deserted, and had to be court-martialed.
The officers said we were cowards and an example had to be set.
Death by firing squad was the verdict the next morning, with no appeal.
So, Mum and Dad, I hope you get this.
Please let my mate's parents know, for he is in no fit state to write.
Trust you and they will understand, as no one here does.

Questions

What do you need to do to make the best of your life?

What should you stop doing and what should you start to do?

STREETS OF HISTORY

The events of history have touched all of our lives. Our language is a result of the people who came from different lands and influenced the way our ancestors spoke. The wars that have devastated the lives of communities over the ages have shaped our culture and ways of life. The explorations that people made to different countries have brought with them new ideas, different kinds of food, and showed us different ways of living.

All of these are what I call Streets Of History. Each one of them provides us with stories from the past, which influence our present. In these stories, we will have a glimpse of how people from Greece, Spain, South Africa, Britain, and other places, have given us different perspectives on life.

Each one of these stories are told in a way that captures particular incidents and events, as if they have come back through the pages of time, to tell us what it was really like, in a world when they did not have computers, jet aeroplanes or the magic of the internet.

A Convict's Denial

Overview

Eleven sailing boats left England in 1787. On board were over 750 convicts. They were being deported to New South Wales, now in the independent country of Australia. However, when they arrived in January 1788, there were no houses, no shops and no modern facilities, such as running water.

Many of the people on these boats, and the ones that arrived later, denied being convicts. Some who were convicted had only stolen a small amount, to provide food and clothing for their family. There were strong feelings of injustice.

This story reflects what I think one of the alleged convicts might have said. But, we must remember most were uneducated and could not write. Even if they had documented their thoughts, who was going to read and listen to their stories? The emerging city of Sydney was over 10,000 miles from their homes in England.

Route of the First Fleet

I pleaded my innocence till my tears ran dry.
The judge said he'd seen my sort many times before:
No job, no home, living life on the fly,
Just another slum dweller from the valley of the poor.
So, they put me on a sailing boat, bound for Sydney Town.
A prisoner of His Majesty, a victim of crime
Sentenced to heavy labour, digging barren ground.
Out of sight, out of mind, forced to serve my time.
Oh, I prayed for truth and justice
Though no one seemed to care.
I was just another convict on the list
Angry beyond compare.
We sailed south, through wind and rain
During the year of 1787 into 1788
Knowing I would never see England again.
That was my convict fate.
Yes, I'm a prisoner of old England,
Innocent of any offence.
But, I can't explain or understand
My exile and 14-year sentence.
But, one day, I'll be free,
Free to make a choice.
Until then, I'll do what I must do.
But, watch they do not catch you.
Oh, yes, beware of the evil traps.
Beware of those who tell lies.
Beware of press gangs.
Beware of Government spies.

Question

Imagine you were one of the convicts of the First Fleet. Write a letter home to your parents, describing the journey and your plans.

Constantine The Great

Overview

How are major ideas developed? In what way are we influenced by values and virtues? After visiting York, in the United Kingdom, and seeing a statue of Emperor Constantine next to York Minster, I asked why?

This story explains how a Roman Emperor changed Western Europe and other parts of the world. It records my imaginary interview with Emperor Constantine The Great who lived from 272AD to 337AD.

Gladiators bestrode the Roman Empire.
Not those in the Coliseum, but in politics.
The death of Caesar was a warning to all:
Stabbed in view of the Senate by his so-called friends.
Who could one trust?
Plots for seizing power defined the Roman Empire.
Colleagues could be more dangerous than foreign enemies.
Command of an army was essential to survival.
Support from high-ranking family members was valuable.
Only then might the Senate bestow its vote in your favour.

Hello, I am Emperor Constantine.
Read on if you want to learn how to survive battles
Not just the physical, but also those that attack your mind.
Learn from my experience.
After all, I wanted to be God's Emperor.
The Almighty's blessing was more important than that of men.
My mother taught me her Christian beliefs.
'Do unto others as they would do unto you,' she said.
Yet, all around me, I witnessed the persecutions.
Many were killed for their beliefs, particularly Christians.
Romans, of course, worshipped many gods,
But, the principles of the Christians impressed me.
Yet, as a soldier amongst soldiers, I said little.
Our job was to protect and extend our Roman Empire.
Barbarians had to be killed, or they would kill us.
My father, an army leader, had told me that from an early age.
In contrast, my mother, a Greek by birth, had a softer approach.
We lived mainly in Serbia until I joined the army.
Then, I was involved in battles on the River Danube and in Asia.
For ten years, and more, I led my troops in many bloody battles.
Diocletian was our Emperor, who ruled from Nicomedia.
When I returned to his Court, in AD 303, I was concerned.
He encouraged the great persecution of Christians.
This was deliberate destruction of people who professed peace.
Without weapons, they were massacred.
It had a big effect on me.
Within two years, Diocletian took ill and retired.
His successor, Galerius, made life difficult for me.
Numerous times his decisions put my life in danger.
Fearing for my life, I escaped during the night.
My father was a ruler in Gaul, so my aim was to join him.
Days and nights of riding, always scared I would be caught.
On arriving, my father said we needed to go to Britannica.
The Picts' tribe and other rebels needed to be defeated.
From our base at Eboracum (York) we went into battle.
On my return, in AD 306, I was told my father was dying.
He conferred on me the supreme title of Augustus.
The Barbarian King Chrocus told his people.
But, would Galerius, with his army, agree?
Would the Senate elders in Rome acknowledge me as Emperor?
After all, I was 1400 miles away.

Rather than returning, I continued our work.
Fighting the northern tribes of Britannica was hard work.
Then, I went to Trier and led our troops against the Franks.
Victories, not hollow words, strengthened my position.
In addition, I ordered new buildings and defences:
Visible means of showing that I was in command.
Word of my leadership achievements reached Rome.
Galerius had to acknowledge my position.
But, in AD 306 a rival, Maxentius seized the Emperor's title.
Could a marriage between our families stop conflict?
Negotiations led me into an arranged marriage with his daughter.
But, even that did not resolve the divisions.
So, I marched my army into battle against the troops of Maxentius.
Romans fighting against Romans and their supporters.
No wonder our enemies saw opportunities!
The Roman Empire had to be unified.
In AD 312, I became the undisputed Emperor of the Western area.
It was during this time, I was more attracted to Christianity.
The philosophy of the Ten Commandments appealed to me.
Ironically, Jesus Christ had been crucified by Romans.
My men asked why we should follow the ideas of a Jew.
After all, had we not defeated them in battle.
I told them the Christian creed spoke to the needs of all.
Therefore, in AD 313, I issued the 'Edict of Milan.'
It provided Christianity protection under the law.
Also, freedom of worship was allowed.
Many of my soldiers took my lead and converted.
But, others kept their own Roman gods.
Each day, we faced danger and death
So, having a faith was a consolation.
Tough men also had fears and anxieties.
My job was to inspire them.
Battles against my rival in the east, Licinius and his troops, were fierce.
After victories in AD 324, I became the undisputed Emperor.
So, I made my policy and plans clear.
In politics, I insisted on unity and allegiance.
In religion, I facilitated Christianity via the 'Nicene Creed.'
In the military, I demanded loyalty and readiness.
In foreign countries, I demanded victory and compliance.
But, what was my purpose?
Many felt it was to make the Roman Empire a Christian one.

There had to be something of value for which to fight.
There had to be a shared set of beliefs.
Better that they be Christian principles than some other creed.
An empire has to have a soul.
So, my message was clear to all.
Live peacefully under Roman law with Christian values.
Constantinople was a shining example of human achievement:
A city proudly named after me.
But, it was difficult to expand and control.
The more territory we gained, the more enemies we created.
The Roman Empire was consistently under attack.
So was I.
At the age of 57, a serious illness descended on me.
It was time for me to be baptised as a Christian.
A Roman leader, but a Christian follower.
It was my time to meet my maker.
I left this world for a better one.
But, in doing so, I had done more than the apostles:
They spread the word, but I authorised it.
As a result, Christianity became the major religion of Europe.

Questions

How have you been influenced by these ideas?

What are the main values you support?

Hadrian

Overview

For centuries, the Romans ruled Europe. They did so by invading territories as far north as the border between England and Scotland. That is one area, amongst many, where they encountered fierce opposition. It is thought that the powerful 9th Legion of the Roman Army was decimated by the northern tribes, who wreaked havoc upon their enemies from the south.

Emperor Hadrian heard of this slaughter, and other defeats, when he gained power. He visited Britain and other European territories and decided it was necessary to develop a new strategy to maintain and develop the Roman Empire.

This is a virtual interview of how he changed the way the Romans ruled in Europe.

Emperors had come to power on the wings of hope.
Emperors had disappeared in divisions of despair.
Not all of them died peacefully in their beds.
Everyone had heard about the assassination of Julius Caesar.
The highest office in the Empire was a dangerous one.

Trajan, my predecessor, had died suddenly on 8th August 117 AD.
My appointment as a Roman Emperor was not by popular vote.
His wife said that he nominated me as his successor.
Would her word carry enough weight in Rome with the Senate?
As Trajan's adopted son, I had his blessing but no documents.
At the time, I was on the field of battle far from Rome.
Securing our borders was my priority.
To do that, I gave up land in Mesopotamia.
Also, I ceded territory to barbarians in Assyria and Armenia:
Better to control a smaller area than lose a larger one.
As well as containing the Arabs, I had to control the Jews.
War on many fronts was difficult and dangerous,
So, I delayed my return to the capital.
News moved at the speed of slow boats and strong horses.
From Syria, it took weeks for me to arrive in Rome.
What reception would I receive?
Although my legions were loyal, senators had power.
After all, my skills were in the field of battle.
Listening to senators babbling was not my theatre.
However, they could legitimise or undermine my role as Emperor.
On arriving in Rome, I found the main point of disagreement:
The majority of Senators wanted the Roman Empire to expand further.
That meant more good Romans would perish.
So, I made my views clear.
We could succeed more effectively by defending, rather than attacking.
After all, conquering additional lands meant further problems.
Our armed forces would be spread too thinly.
Our supply lines would become longer.
Our enemies watched and were waiting.
Let us not over stretch ourselves, I told the senators.
Peace through strength was my motto.
Immediately, there were accusations.
Had I lost the will to fight?
Ironic, as I had made my name as a warrior for the Empire.
Within a short time, my worst fears were realised.
News from Britannia arrived.
The Brigantes people in the north had attacked our 9th Legion.
Major losses of men and material were reported.
As Emperor, I needed to assess and control the situation.
Therefore, legions were prepared for the long voyage.
Travelling at about 20 miles a day was hard work.

The journey took about three months.
On arrival, in 122 AD, I received grave news:
I was told that our 9th Legion had been wiped out.
Should I risk losing more men by retaliating?
A new approach was needed.
A line of defence was required.
I gave the order to build what became known as Hadrian's Wall.
Defence was the best form of attack.
Similar plans were implemented on the Rhine and Danube Rivers.
Yes, building was important to me.
On my return to Rome, I pressed ahead with new constructions:
The Pantheon and Temple of Venus were classic buildings.
But, I spent more time with my troops than in Rome.
Living with them in the fields of battle was more to my taste,
Though some expeditions were horrific.
In Judea, it was estimated half a million were killed.
My troops destroyed more than 50 towns.
Likewise, in Arabic areas, we imposed control.
If we had not done so we would have been massacred.
On my travels, I enjoyed visiting Greece.
Their culture and language appealed to me.
But, protecting the Roman Empire was my main task.
Power was based on judgement.
Asking questions, gaining data and making decisions.
Negotiation often proved a better option than war.
Maintaining the peace was difficult.
Defeated tribes wanted revenge.
How could I gain both control and co-operation?
In Rome, I developed an improved legal code.
In doing so, I encouraged masters to treat their slaves properly.
Life could be brutal for so many.
We needed to assist those who helped us.
But, our enemies could not expect any mercy.
Those who complied gained benefits.
After all, we were leaders in technology.
Our builders created magnificent buildings.
Our culture and education led the world.
In all, I was Emperor for 21 years.
An exciting time, when I supported new ideas.
Pax Romana.
Art and architecture to reflect our culture.

Power, not just to conquer, but to create.
We could develop a new world order?
But, for how long?
No one lasts forever.
But, I wondered, could our Roman Empire do so?

Questions

If you were a Roman Emperor at the time when Hadrian ruled, would you have continued to expand by conquering more territory, or would you have consolidated and defended the existing borders?

What, in your opinion, were the major leadership characteristics of Emperor Hadrian?

Patagonian Welsh

Overview

Why do people migrate from one country to another? There are many amazing stories of people who chose to leave the land of their birth and settle in another country, despite all the risks and challenges they faced in order to survive.

This story relates to the brave Welsh colonists, who left the valleys and villages of their homeland in 1865, to settle in Argentina.

Fear can inspire amazing achievements.
Dreams can provide astounding motivation.
In many Welsh villages, both fear and dreams existed.
The industrial revolution changed the traditional way of life.
Most of the young people went to work in the towns.
Their parents and the family members remained behind.
Farming declined and shops shut.
There were fewer students in the schools.
'Welsh' Wales was in decline.
Could the language and way of life be saved?
Many people felt depressed, resigned to the inevitable.
But, not Michael D Jones.
Born in a village near Bala, North Wales, he spoke out.
Seeing his Welsh culture decline made him angry.

He was a minister of the gospel and had a vision.
'Why, not establish a Welsh colony?' he asked.
'Where would that be?' asked members of his chapel.
'Patagonia', he replied.
'Where in Britain is that?' enquired one of the congregation.
'It's in Argentina, South America,' he responded.
A ripple of laughter went round the group.
'Have you been there to see what it is like?'
'No,' said Michael, 'but I have heard that it is beautiful.'
Michael had only been to North America.
With enthusiasm, he told the congregation of his grand idea.
Welsh culture could be protected in a new land.
Through his contacts an opportunity was created.
The Argentine Government said it would provide land for colonists.
So, the wild idea began to take shape.
When Jones' wife inherited money, funds became available.
A boat, called the *Mimosa*, was acquired.
For months, discussions took place.
Across the valleys and hills the message was carried.
At meetings, in chapels and shops, the word spread.
Patagonia could be the 'promised land',
A place where Welsh people could feel safe,
Where the language and culture would have a future.
Amazingly, Jones gained enough people to sign up.
On 28th May 1865, the *Mimosa* set sail.
On board were 153 courageous settlers.
But Michael Jones was not on board.
He continued his religious work in Wales.
The colonists set sail from Liverpool.
Two months later, they arrived at a place called Port Madryn.
The dream of a Welsh colony met the harsh reality:
Strangers in a strange land.
Communication problems arose, as the locals spoke Spanish.
It was cold and there were no houses.
Travelling inland was slow and water was scarce.
The colonists worked hard to survive.
Settling in the Chubut River Valley was a major decision.
It gave them access to water.
But, the ground all around was hard to farm.
There were over 30 young children amongst the settlers.

In contrast, only four were over the age of 40.
With enthusiasm, the band of young Welsh colonists started work.
Basic houses and a chapel were built.
Berwyn Mathews and Lewis Jones led the way.
The settlers survived with help from the local Indian tribes.
They knew how to fish and hunt.
The Welsh also wanted to farm the land.
Understandings were reached, initially, by sign language.
Trading depended on growing crops.
Long hours of back-breaking work were required,
But, not on Sundays.
The Sabbath was respected at chapel services.
So it was that the Welsh developed the Chubut Valley.
Democracy was established.
Welsh colonial women were the first in the country to gain a vote.
Indeed, one of their women made a breakthrough innovation.
Mrs Jenkins suggested a planned irrigation system.
With water the valley became green, with a good supply of food.
New emigrants from Wales arrived until interrupted by the 1st World War.
The settlements of Rawson and Trelew became small towns.
So it was that the Welsh became part of Argentina.
A way of life that continues today.

Questions

If you were to leave your country, what other land would you choose to settle in?

What would be the main factors that would determine your decision to move to another land?

Prisoner President

Overview

During 2017, I visited Robben Island, Cape Town, South Africa, and was given a tour of the jail where Nelson Mandela was imprisoned. The guide was a fellow political prisoner, who was there at the same time as the man who would become the President of South Africa.

It takes between 30-60 minutes to reach the island on a boat. Therefore, prisoners had few visitors. The living conditions were very basic and the work was hard. These are my thoughts on the experience.

The cell had not changed.
No bed, just a mat on the floor.
No heating, just one blanket.
No toilet, just a bucket.
No chair or desk.
No escape from the island prison.
27 years served,
Hard labour in a quarry,
Punishment for political protest.
Today, I am inside one of the cells.
Outside the bars is one of the former inmates,
Another victim of Apartheid in South Africa,

Imprisoned here on Robben Island, near Cape Town
Alongside the future President.
He talks quietly about the experience.
'It was our University,' he says.
'Few of us had formal higher education.
We learned with and from each other.'
Outside, we see the exercise yard, surrounded by high walls.
Beyond is the quarry of hard labour.
The sun beats down.
'There was little food or water.
We survived by helping each other,' he said.
The future President was made to work as a slave.
No pay.
No holidays.
No escape.
Until the negotiations.
Was it too late?
The plans had been discussed.
Democracy would prevail,
The rule of law upheld,
Reconciliation pursued.
So said the new President.
Peace rather than war
After 27 years in prison.

Questions

To what extent is the legacy of Nelson Mandela being upheld today?

What are your views about punishment for political protests?

Robin Hood

Overview

People in every country develop heroes. The British love the story of Robin Hood, but who was he really?

He lived sometime between 1200 and 1300 AD. That was a time when Britain had been invaded and was controlled by the French. Some say that Robin Hood had fought in the Middle East crusades. Upon his return, he found that his family land had been stolen. He became a significant figure in folk history, and there are many songs and stories about his exploits. Here is my interpretation.

Like Jesus, I had my band of merry men.
Like Jesus, I had a cause.
Like Jesus, my name lives on.
They say I was an outlaw.
But, that is an outrageous myth.
A distortion of the truth.
I was a freedom fighter for my people:
I led the Anglo Saxons.
We fought against William the Conqueror's Norman invaders.
They had killed my countrymen and taken our land.

We were victims in a French colony.
William crowned himself King of England.
He wanted to impose his language and Gallic ways upon us.
They say I robbed the rich to feed the poor.
I certainly robbed the French to care for my people.
Yet, what goes around comes around.
Within 200 years, the boot was on the other foot.
My countrymen, the English, invaded France.
They won many battles and claimed much land
Before Joan of Arc showed the French men how to fight:
Esprit de corps winning over the stronger force.
I remained a thorn in the side of the so called King.
I was the real King of the people.
If elections had been possible, I would have walked in.
Now I am a mythical figure in history.
Forgotten are the issues, other than by a few.
But England still has a monarch,
Ironically of German descent.
France no longer has a King.
Nor did William the Conqueror become King of France.
It is a peculiar world.

Questions

Who are the heroes in your life?

What are you doing to fight for what you believe is right?

Sarmatians In Britain

Overview

Conquerors dictate the terms. The Romans often made their victims march thousands of miles to control the tribes in new territories, which they had gained through battle. This story describes a little known example of how a defeated army was conscripted to subdue and guard people in Britain. So began a migration which changed so many lives in different ways.

We were a proud people.
For centuries, we had defended our lands.
Indeed, with victories our territories expanded.
We occupied over 5000 miles of grasslands from Hungary to China.
Our common language was derived from Iran.
Originally, we lived on the east side of the River Don.
In the 3rd century BC our warriors defeated the Scythians.
It was the start of many other conquests.
In the next 300 years we spread southwards.
Although we had success, it was the start of a great calamity.
The Romans suffered as a result of our raids.
Eventually, Emperor Marcus Aurelius organised his troops to attack us.
Over 8000 of our men were captured.
In AD 179 he offered us a deal.

We would be killed, or we could support the Roman Army.
Our leaders decided it best to accept their offer.
So it was that 5500 and more of our best men were sent to Britannia.
It was no easy journey, as we marched across Europe.
Roman troops did us no favours, as we had been their enemies.
Known as 'auxiliaries' we were battle hardened troops.
Many took ill on the way and we had to bury some of our best soldiers.
Even when we reached Britannia, we marched another 300 miles.
Our initial job was to defend Hadrian's Wall against invaders from the north.
Bitterly cold in winter, and windy with rain for most of the year.
We were pleased when the Romans said we were going south.
'Where to?' we asked.
'Ribchester,' the Commander of the Legion replied.
'You will help our Chester garrison to guard the North West,' he explained.
We arrived around the year AD 200, about 50 miles north of Chester.
As well as military work, our digging skills were required.
In addition to extending the fort, homes and a bath house had to be built.
Many people think that the Romans conquered Britannia.
Yes, in terms of the invasion and the military control.
In reality, it was our troops and similar ones that did the hard work.
We controlled the areas on their behalf.
Local people accepted they could not defeat the mighty Romans,
So did we.
What was the point of rebelling?
To return home would take weeks of walking.
Our people had been defeated.
On the way, we would be attacked and killed by local tribes.
Despite our grumbles, we honoured the deal with the Romans.
In doing so, we could claim Roman citizenship after 25 years of service.
I was one of them, stationed at Bremetanacum Veteranorum.
The veterans on the hill, as we were known.
We lived at the Roman Fort on the River Ribble.
So, it was that men of the Euro-Asian steppes met Britannia girls.
That is how we came to learn the local language.
Of course, the relationships led to many births.
Those that decided to live together became families.
I was one who chose a civil marriage with my local girlfriend.
Upon retirement, I was allocated land by the Romans.
This had been taken from the Brigantes tribe, whom they had defeated.
So it was that I became a farmer instead of a fighter.

I was one of the first Euro-Asian immigrants to make Britannia my home.
My children were of mixed descent and spoke three languages.
They learned Latin, also my native language and the local tongue.
I hoped they would have a better life than my own.

Questions

What do you think were the major effects of the Roman invasion of Britain, on the lives of the local people?

How did the Romans manage to control such vast areas of land and the people who lived there?

The Door

Overview

When I departed on a cruise holiday, I never expected to stumble on a historic story that has changed the lives of many people. After a few days cruising, we arrived in Germany. There was an opportunity to visit Wittenberg, an old town that is steeped in tradition.

Our guide told us that Martin Luther, the great religious reformer, had lived in the town. It was here that he wrote his denunciation of the Roman Catholic priests, for selling indulgences to 'forgive' people for their sins. Indeed, people could buy the indulgence, a form of remission of a sin, before they had committed the sin. Luther said that the Roman Catholic Church was being run like a business. Priests were making lots of money, rather than concentrating on their parish duties.

So, in 1517, he wrote 95 theses and posted them on the door of the Wittenberg Cathedral. That was an act of defiance and rebellion that changed history. So, while in Wittenberg, I decided to conduct a virtual interview, reflecting on what I think Martin Luther would have said.

For nights I lay awake.
It can't be right, it cannot be true.
Selling the forgiveness of sins.
Didn't Christ drive out the money changers from the temple?
Did he not say that only the Almighty can forgive sins?

Why then should people pay for an indulgence?
Salvation cannot be bought by metal.
Redemption of the soul cannot be traded like a commodity.
It is a crime that is being committed in the name of the Faith.
Prostitution of forgiveness is no different than prostitution of the body.
Why should a rich person have more access to heaven than a poor man?
Payments are even made before the crimes are committed.
Tetzel offers indulgences in advance, like gold plated insurance.
It can't be right, it can't be true.
The Ten Commandments are now negotiable.
Commit any sin you want for a price, all comers welcome.
The Catholic Church is selling snake oil to line the pockets of those in power.
The Pope and his priests are conspiring with criminals.
They are committing fraud and must be held to account.
Tonight I will challenge the wrong doers and write the truth.
Forgiveness cannot be bought.
Salvation is a gift.
True confession and personal penance, not indulgences, are the answer.
It is the Almighty who is the truth, the light and the way.
There is no need for a priest to intercede.
Each person, without fee, can make their own confession.
Jesus Christ said we should be in constant penance.
So, tonight there will be no sleep until the word is written.
Tomorrow I will post the Theses at Wittenberg Cathedral,
Not inside, just for the faithful, but outside, for all the world to see.
Let all who see the message act to save their souls
And spread the word of truth of what is written on The Door.

Questions

What are the issues that you feel it is important to protest about?

To what extent have you protested and in what ways?

The Greeks

Overview

The Greeks are famous for developing one of the great civilisations. We remember their outstanding philosophers and writers. But, who are the Greeks?

This story captures the messages of many of their citizens, who contributed to our understanding of social life in the early days.

This is our story
About how we came to be.
Leaders of the ancient world,
Famous in history.
In the mists of time on Mount Olympus
We learned of a God called Zeus.
Powerful as thunder, he became our ruler.
With him we could not lose.
On Mount Helicon lived the muses,
Who were daughters of King Zeus.
Goddesses of art and science
Guiding our ideas and views.
But, the gods were myths of our mind
And problems needed solutions.
So, our philosophers used logic and time
To guide us beyond illusions.
Socrates and Plato led the way
In schools of education.
Teaching students every day,
Giving them inspiration.
Yes, we are the Greeks.
Our people wanted peace.
But, city States fought each other,
Bringing tears to many a mother's eye.
We also started the Olympics,

A festival of sport and fun.
There, we competed with swords and sticks
And gave laurels to those who won.
We had many scientists who did experiments.
Instead of guessing, they collected evidence.
Their research was based on samples.
Here are some important examples.
When Archimedes sat in his bath,
Watching the water, he had a laugh.
'It rises,' he said, 'by my body weight
So, that is a law of nature, I state.'
'My name is Euclid and I explained the Elements.
So, mathematics and geometry made more sense.'
Also, Pythagoras invented his theorem
Since when, students have feared him.
Aristotle linked science to philosophy
That widened what we see.
'I agree with that', said Hippocrates.
'It will help us fight and beat disease.'
Our patron saint we called Athena.
Though no one has ever seen her.
We looked to her for our protection
At a temple called the Parthenon.
It was started in 447 BC
Long before you and me.
High on a famous hill
You will see our Acropolis citadel.
So join with us and share our history
From the mountain gods to democracy.
From ancients wars to Olympic Games,
Let's give thanks to our famous names.

Questions

What learning points from this story do you feel are important?

To what extent have the Greeks influenced our life today?

The Spaniard

Overview

After making a tour of southern Spain in the spring of 2016, I became very interested in the history and traditions of the country. It is a mixture of what the native born people have gained from invaders. The Phoenicians, the Romans, the Moors, and many more, have left their mark.

My short story reflects a glimpse of an exciting country and how one person tells the story.

They arrived in force and took our land.
Their soldiers took our women.
Living off the land, they took our food.
Stealing whatever they found, it was sold back to us at high prices.
We thought they would move on after a short time.
Instead more of them arrived.
Proclamations were made that we had to obey their laws.
Taxes were imposed and we had to pay, or suffer punishments.
Their architects arrived with their soldiers.
We had to build in the style that they designed.
Soon, we became servants in our own land.
Previously, we had been invaded by the Phoenicians.
They seemed to be mainly traders.
The Romans arrived later and stayed for centuries.
It was a military invasion designed to extend The Roman Empire.
Centurions led their men and protected areas they conquered.
Walls were built to defend their ill-gotten gains.
Next, they started to send our fruit and vegetables to their markets.

All of the time, they demanded that we develop the land.
So, their invasion continued for hundreds of years.
They brought their language and culture.
Amphitheatres for sport and pleasure were built.
Within their walled towns, they established forums and plazas.
The Romans brought culture and organisation.
We watched them go to the Roman Baths.
It seemed like a religious ritual, as if they were going to church.
Eventually, the Romans were driven out.
Visigoth invaders from the north arrived.
They focused more on rape and pillage.
Visigoths were takers not givers.
A lot of painful lessons were learned.
Our ancestors had to endure a lot of insults and injuries.
Messages were passed down from one generation to another.
Other invaders made us realise we needed to be strong.
We knew our time would come.
So, we were ready when Columbus discovered South America.
We took what we had learned, through pain and suffering.
We knew what to do.
The only way to succeed was by force.
Cortes and Pizarro imposed brutal leadership.
The local tribes had little defence against swords.
Against sickness and disease, they had no immunity.
Ironically, we imposed Roman Catholicism for their salvation.
But, there were few to be saved after the starvation.
Yes, the legacy of the priests remains in every country in South America.
Also, Spanish is the language of all those countries, except one.
Yes, we learned a lot about how to build an Empire from the Romans.
But, like theirs, it did not last.
So, what will be the future?

Questions

Is illegal immigration invasion by another name? What should be done to stop it?

What examples do you have where invasions have changed the country and in what way?

STREETS OF WORK

We all learn a lot from our experience at work, that we never learned when we were at school. Indeed, each job that we do defines us as much as we try to undertake the role that we are given. In the process, we begin to understand not only who we are, but who we can become.

The stories in The Streets Of Work reflect many of the people I have met in the jobs that I have done. They also reflect those I have met, who were working to help me on the road of life. As I travelled from one place to another, and stayed at hotels, I learned a lot about their work and their attitudes to life. Some were happy, as they felt they had made the right choices. Others were sad, because they had regrets, and felt that opportunities had passed them by. All of them had insights based on their experiences. I have tried to capture these, by writing the story as if the individual concerned is giving me a personal interview.

You will meet people who had important jobs, such as 'The Royal Fool'. The story of 'The Concierge' will show how someone who is not well paid can have considerable influence, and hold many secrets. In contrast, there are people who are committed to helping others through their beliefs, but may have the same problems as those they advise. You will also meet 'The Funny Man', who professes laughter and fun, but also reflects on the side of his life that may not be so happy. All of these stories can help us to understand our own lives, through the experiences of others.

Actress

Overview

In life, as Shakespeare famously noted, we all play many roles, despite not being professional actors.

Too many people are locked into a job or circumstances which do not enable them to flourish and develop their inherent talent. For others, they shine on the public stage of theatre or politics, but behind the mask they lead a very different life.

This is a story of one such person that I met on the road of life.

You set your store by acting
And you knew you could not fail.
For behind the mask you have confidence
To share and tell the tale.
But once outside the limelight
No longer centre stage.
There's solitude and loneliness.
And you play a different game.
For who are you?
And who am I?
And what part do we play?
Will we be tomorrow, what we are today?
I sense the world is not the stage
On which you can perform
With its many disappointments.

The lull before the storm.
You need to have a theatre
Where drama is controlled.
So that you can be yourself
And really play your role.
You are a gifted actress.
You know your lines so well.
But, in the story of your life
You have far more to tell.
So, join the play and you will see
The way we are today.
Oh, what is real and what is true
When there's only you and me?

Questions

We all play a role in the theatre of life. Identify the main roles you play in your own life.

Which of these roles complement your own talents?

Coffee Pickers

Overview

A visit to Costa Rica helped me see life from a different perspective.

Although the name implies 'rich' coast or country, many of the people are very poor. Travelling into the countryside as a tourist, I saw the people working hard in the fields.

This story was written as a result of what I observed.

Their bodies, burnt by the sun, will take another battering today.
A fierce heat is already radiating from the ground.
Pedro, with clothes of rough cloth and boots much worn, leads his
family.
His hat, wrinkled by the sun, perched lightly on his head.
His wife follows, a child in one arm, a basket in the other.
This is a family team.
They have two girls under ten years and two boys, barely teenagers.
They move into the fields.
They strip the beans from the coffee trees
With silver sharp fingers so fast the eye cannot see.
Moving, with hardly a pause between the rows,
They pick the beans in silence.
Their baskets are filled, but not their pockets or their stomachs.
The sun beats down, a blessing or a curse?

It is the lifeblood that supports their meagre purse.
At night, it is cold as they sleep in their hovels.
No light shines until dawn, when the coffee fields call.
An ever-growing band of immigrants compete for their work.
It is an existence, a way of life, a living.
They are still a family, more so than many they serve.
Here, in Costa Rica, they collect the beans for our cups.
Far away, in cafes, we enjoy the coffee they provide.
We talk and drink, but of their life, what do we think?

Question

How would you describe the interest you have in your job?

Concierge

Overview

On my travels I stay at many hotels. The first person that I usually meet is the hotel porter or receptionist. In some hotels, such a person may be called 'a concierge', if they also assist with information, as well as helping with one's luggage.

This is the story of a person who has welcomed many people to the hotel where he works. He prefers to be known as 'a concierge.'

I am the person guests first meet when they arrive at our hotel.
Whatever my problems, it is important that I give them a positive
welcome:
A warm smile, a confident handshake and help with their luggage.
That is what people remember.
First impressions count.
So do last impressions.
I am the person who says 'good bye,'
'Adios,' 'au revoir' and 'look forward to seeing you again.'
In between those two events, I learn a lot.
It is not that I have to be inquisitive.
Indeed, it is the guests who pose the questions.
My job is to find solutions in a discreet kind of way.
Many of the requests are similar:
'Where can I find the museum, or a book on the local history?'
As the sun sets on another day, the questions become more interesting.

Of course, when people are with a group they want to have a good time.
A pub tour for the guys is always a favourite.
However, I know that can mean trouble five or six hours later.
These days, the women on 'hen's parties' can be heavy drinkers.
Increasingly, they want to bring back the men they meet
to continue the party.
We have always had the men bringing back the women they meet.
Now, with so-called equal rights, opportunities abound.
Maybe eyes used to be raised when men returned with boyfriends.
Now, there are more than a few women who return
with their girlfriends.
Of course, if they pay for the room it is their business.
We are not there to approve or disapprove.
My orders are simply to ensure there is no disturbance to other guests.
The next morning it is hard to tell who is who.
Some leave in the early hours,
Others stay over for breakfast, providing they pay.
My job is to see all, hear all, and say nothing.
Discretion is a key skill in my job,
Particularly, of course, with the punters.
They arrive in force on the horse racing days.
Gambling is a way of life for many.
In the old days, I was known as the 'bookies' runner.'
Punters would give me money to bet on a race.
If they won, they were generous.
With the arrival of the internet, I no longer play that role.
But, there are other ways to make extra money.
Florists and hairdressers know I can market their services.
They give me a reward for promotions that lead to sales.
Taxi drivers show appreciation when I call them regularly.
Restaurant owners have arrived with cash in sealed envelopes
After I have sent a group to their place for dinner.
Tour operators have also rewarded me for recommendations.
Direct tips can more than double my wage.
Of course, the operators of brothels will always pay to get business.
The local casino likes me to hand out their leaflets.
But, what about day to day tips?
Are they important?
Americans, Arabs and big rollers from Asia,
can make my job very worthwhile.
They pay the most and demand the least.

They know that I can be helpful in many ways.
But they like to show they have power to command.
It can become tricky when they want personal information
on their rivals.
So, I am careful to choose the assignments that I take.
After all, what is money worth if you do not have safety?
People may think I have a simple job.
After all, I do not have an advanced education.
But, I earn more than many who do.
Nor do I have specialist technical skills, like an engineer or a chef.
I meet and greet clients.
Carrying their luggage, I show them to their room.
It is the start of a relationship.
As a concierge, I am there to be helpful.
Many people recognise the relationship we share can beneficial.
In my job, it is whom you know, not what you know, that counts.

Question

Who are the people who most help you when you are travelling?

Father Confessor

Overview

On a tour of southern France, I rented a car and decided to stop off at the small villages and towns *en route*. In one of them, my attention was drawn to an old church standing in the centre of the market place. I walked inside. It was empty except for the priest. We did not speak, but I imagined what he might have been thinking, as he had just finished hearing a confession.

We are trained to hear confessions.
But each time I am surprised by what I hear.
Today was an example.
A woman of about 40 years of age came to make her confession.
'What is it that you wish to say?' I asked.
After a few general statements, she came to the point.
'I want to leave my husband,' she said with feeling.
'Has he been unfaithful?' I enquired.
'No, to the contrary,
He works hard, as a bricklayer.
He comes home every night when he has finished work.'
'Does he beat you?' I asked, looking for a reason.
'No,' she replied.
'In that respect, he is a perfect husband.'

'So, why do you want to leave him?' I asked.
'He is boring,' she replied with feeling.
I was about to say that was not a basis for divorce
But, I realised that there was probably more to the story.
'What does he do that bores you?' I enquired.
'The issue is mainly in the bedroom,' she replied, looking downward.
I knew this was going to be difficult:
By the nature of my vows, I had no experience in such matters.
'What is the problem?' I asked.
I tried to convey an air of compassion and authority.
'We have been married over 20 years.
I want a child and time is against me,' she said, looking downward again.
'Is your husband against the idea?' I asked.
'I do not think he is capable,' she said, with tears falling down her cheeks.
'How do you know?' I enquired.
'I have had tests, but he refuses,' she replied.
Now, I knew for sure, this was not an ordinary confession.
What should I say?
No sin had yet been committed.
Penance was not appropriate.
'Have you considered adopting a child?' I asked.
Grasping for an answer, I knew was not going to work.
'I want my own baby,' she said, in a forceful way.
'It is my natural right as a woman,' she added.
'That is why I am on this Earth.'
'The Almighty may not agree with that,' I said.
Immediately, I knew that was the wrong thing to say.
Her sobbing from the other side of the confessional box was uncontrollable.
Some minutes elapsed, which gave me time to think.
'Have you told your husband what you have told me?' I asked.
'No, I thought it best to gain your guidance,' she replied.
'Do you have another man with whom you have a relationship?' I asked.
'Not at present,' she said.
'But, I have started to look at internet sites that make introductions.'
At last, I thought, the admission of intent to sin.
Should I focus on that and give her a warning?
As a Catholic, all of her life, she knew the Commandments.
She had not come to confession to receive a lecture.
And what right, as a priest, did I have to condemn her actions?
She was confronting real life issues about her purpose and identity.
The issues were as much psychological and biological

as of religious concern.
I think that she realised I was in a dilemma.
She looked upward.
'I think it best if I pray about the situation,' she said.
'Yes,' I said, feeling relieved.
'Please come and see me again after your prayers,' I added.
'I will,' she said and left the church by the side door
into the pouring rain.

Questions

What advice would you give to this lady?

What are the principles that influence your way of life?

Funny Man

Overview

Those who become comedians and make other people laugh, often have sadness and melancholy in their own lives.

As performers, their lives are a contrast with their outward persona and actions making our lives happier, while internally, their own worries are hidden out of our sight.

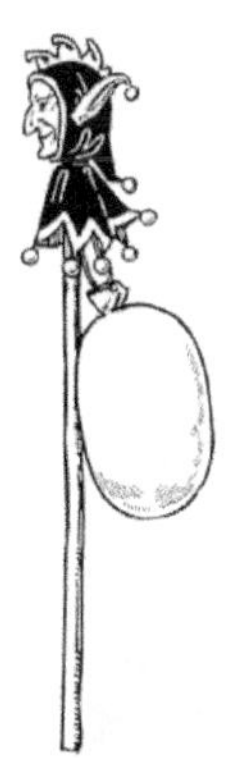

Roll up roll up!
The show is about to begin.
Come on in and enjoy yourself.
You're welcome, come on in.
I travel far, for many miles.
To tell my jokes and see their smiles.
'Cos, I'm the Funny Man!
I've a painted face and bright red nose,
A big blue hat and baggy clothes.
Yes, I'm the Funny Man!
I tell a tale, I sing a song
And I play the fool, all day long.
'Cos, I'm the Funny Man!
I hear them cheer and I see them cry.
I feel for them and so I try
To be the Funny Man!
I'm a jester, who likes the sun

And a joker, wild, having fun.
Yes, I'm the Funny Man!
I see them come, I see them go.
I read their faces, that's how I know.
I'm the Funny Man!
I'm a comic, I'm a clown.
Sometimes up and sometimes down.
But, always ready with a joke.
Even though I may be broke.
'Cos, I'm the Funny Man!

Question

Why are some people who purport to be funny in real life rather sad?

Life Saver

Overview

It is natural and normal to have anxieties, from time to time, about one's health. We know that it is almost impossible to live beyond 100 years. But, how can we extend our life beyond the average of people from a similar background to us? This story reflects an interesting conversation, which may be helpful.

Rushing to the train, I wondered if I would get a seat.
Luckily, there was just one unoccupied.
Out of breath, I sat down next to a middle-aged man in a suit.
He looked up and said, 'Well, you've had your exercise for the day.'
The train pulled out of the station on our long journey southwards.
'Yes,' I said, panting, while trying to get air into my lungs.
'Although, I am not sure that will do me any good.'
'Every bit counts,' he said with a smile.
My pulse was racing at probably 100 beats a minute or more.
'My job doesn't demand much physical exertion,' I replied.
'What do you do?' he asked.
'I write books and articles on education,' I said.
'And what about yourself?' I enquired.
'A doctor,' he replied in a low voice, as if it was a secret not to be shared.
'Then, you save people's lives.'
'No, priests and ministers of the gospel try to do that,' he said with a quiet laugh.
'But, as a doctor of medicine, you are trained to save lives?' I replied.
'In emergencies, it may be possible,' he replied, as if there was no certainty.
The train had now picked up speed.
Fields of golden corn flashed by.
'Only you can save your life,' he said gravely.

'What do you mean?' I asked.
'Exercise is the key to a long life,' he said.
'If you walk a few miles per day it makes a big difference.'
On average, it means an extra year of life.
Playing golf has major health benefits.'
'Surely that creates stress when you don't play well,' I said with a laugh.
'Maybe, but two rounds a week adds five years to your life,' he replied.
'I don't play golf,' I said, 'but I do walk a lot.'
'Good,' he replied, 'but make sure it is at least 30 minutes a day.'
'What else can I do to save my own life?'
'Eat fish a couple of times a week and also vegetables.
Reduce foods that cause diabetes and cholesterol.'
'You mean cut the sugar and fat in my diet?' I said.
'Yes, and keep alcohol to one or two drinks per day.'
'Sounds as if I will save money, if I work on saving my life.
What else should I do?' I asked.
'Wash your hands regularly to keep bacteria at bay,' he said.
'Particularly, when you have been handling money,' he added.
'In that case, I know a man who saved millions of lives,' I stated.
'William Lever made and sold soap from about 1890 onwards.
That reduced infections.'
'Well,' said the doctor, 'he is a real hero.
So was Dr Louis Pasteur, who taught us about the dangers of bacteria.
Likewise, Dr Lister showed us how to reduce bacterial infection.
That was a breakthrough in saving lives.'
The train was starting to slow down.
People picked up their cases.
'It was good to meet you,' I said to the doctor.
'And you also,' he replied.
'I won't shake hands,' he said.
'Too many bacteria being exchanged.'
'Understood,' I replied, 'I am off to save my life.'

Questions

What do you plan to do to make the best of your life in the years you have remaining?

Specifically, what will you do to improve the way you eat, drink, and participate in exercise?

Royal Fool

Overview

As a psychologist, I have long been interested in how people communicate. George Bernard Shaw, the great writer, said - 'The single biggest problem with communication is the illusion that it has taken place.'

Those in high positions often have problems with communication as they feel messages are filtered and diluted before they are heard. To improve his perceptions, King Henry VIII of England appointed William Somers as his Court Jester.

This story is based on my perceptions of those times. As we say, many a truth is told in jest. This is how I imagine the King would have told the story.

Who could we trust to tell the truth?
Most of them were parrots.
They repeated exactly what they heard.
True or false, they did not question.
Some were manipulators.
They told me that which would advance their cause:
No better than the seducers.
They appealed to my vices.
Of course, the priests promised salvation if I repented,
Hoping they could profit from their flattery,
Appealing to my virtues rather than my vices.
Negotiators came with deals, bearing promises of silver and gold
Usually better in the presentation than the production.
Lords of the Realm competed for favours.

They always wanted more power than their rivals.
Even members of my Court were not reliable.
Too many years in self-serving jobs.
Lacking contact with the masses, they were out of touch.
But, how well did I understand the ordinary people?
Many were Catholics.
Between 1536 and 1540 I closed down their places of worship.
At the same time, I appointed myself Head of the English Church.
Absolute power requires absolute obedience.
I needed information to root out opponents.
So it was that I searched for someone with little to lose.
My courtiers and guards wanted to protect me.
Rightly so, as I had many enemies, in addition to the religious fanatics.
However, could I trust the protectors?
Fear consumed me, as I remembered the history of Rome.
Caesar was felled by those he knew well.
Was there a Brutus at my door?
If so, who would tell me?
Each night, I lay worrying.
The whining wind sent more than shivers up my spine.
Weird noises filled the old castle building with creaks and groans.
The next day, I attended a local fair to support a Protestant charity.
A jester was entertaining people.
Dressed in many colours, he told captivating tales.
Could he be my eyes and ears?
I asked my courier to bring him to my royal tent.
'You have talent,' I told him.
'Sire, I am but a simple jester,' he replied.
'That is what I need at my Court,' I told him.
'What do you want me to do?' he asked.
'You will be my Royal Fool,' I said.
'Sire, it will be an honour,' he replied.
'You will entertain me, once a week,' I told him.
That is how I discovered the mood of the people.
The jester, while playing the fool, reflected the realities.
His stories told me what I needed to know.
There was wisdom in his wit and satire.
Many a truth is spoken in jest.
In addition, he told me of the gossip.
The word on the street, reflected the plots of the Court.
More truths are spoken with drink.

So, it was that I paid for his merriment.
At events, he let it be known what I wanted to be known.
We had an understanding.
His jesting helped me focus on my enemies.
So it was that we trusted each other.
Every King needs a fool to forecast the future.
The Royal Fool was my Royal Spy.

Questions

Who tells you the truth, and who tells you what you want to hear?

How do you distinguish between truth and fiction?

Teacher

Overview

We have all had teachers who stick in our memories for good reasons or otherwise. At a young age, we are more impressionable. When I went to school, there could be 30 students in a class. Often, the teacher spent most time trying to control those who were not easily conditioned.

But, one teacher had been at the school for a long time. She had taught my mother. So, by the time I arrived at the school, she knew all about control. More than that, she knew about the practical psychology of day-to-day school life. So, this is what I think she would have said, if I had returned to the school and interviewed her.

I have seen them come and go.
Over 30 years, I have done my best to give them the basics.
Reading, writing and arithmetic.
You cannot go far without those.
But, they are only the basic skills.
Of far more importance, in the long run, are the character factors.
For example, is it better to comprehend quickly, or to persevere?
Some students could do both, but not all of them.
Indeed, those who quickly got the message often became bored.
They did not explore the issues in depth.
Seeking more stimulation, they moved on to other topics.
Those who had perseverance kept going
Until they mastered the subject in some depth.
That led me to consider different types of learners.
From an early age I could see those who preferred width,
While others preferred depth.

I also reflected on the process of learning.
All of the students had learned to speak English
before they attended school.
Therefore, they did not have formal lessons.
They had imitated what they heard.
Then, they repeated what they heard many times.
Imitation, repetition and application, in my view, are the keys to learning.
Also, I think that I learnt as much from my students as they did from me.
Trying to discover their special talent and develop it was a major task.
Mozart knew, by the age of five, that he was destined to be a musician.
Shakespeare realised that to develop his talent
he needed to move to London,
Which he did in about 1588, at the age of 24.
So, given these examples, my approach was to give the students projects.
Applying ideas is the main way we can assess our interests.
That was the challenging and interesting aspect of my work.
I became more of a facilitator of learning.
Helping students to help each other was the essential element.
Learning with and from others, not just from books, was important.
Projects taught the students about teamwork.
Some of them came from homes with little support.
Others, in my view, where given too much.
They had everything they wanted and more.
Discussion of their work, as a team, was vital to learning.
After all, for the rest of their lives they will depend on others in teams.
As a teacher, I saw students learning how to make decisions.
Judgement came not just from knowledge, but experience and perception.
We can travel to gain experience, but conception requires thought.
I asked students to keep a record of keywords and use them.
As a teacher, I know there are very few right answers.
So often the answers depend on probabilities.
People who are risk averse will not want to make a decision.
My job was to help each child develop their levels of confidence.
They could all continue learning if they were determined and persistent.

Questions

Who is the teacher that you remember most clearly, and why?

Who are the people that have had an influence on your life, and in what way?

The Persian

Overview

People who drive taxis usually have interesting stories to tell. They meet people from all sectors of the community. As a result of what they see and hear each day, they are usually well informed on a wide array of topics.

Many of the new taxi drivers are immigrants. In Germany, I met one who called himself a Persian. As he drove me from Frankfurt Airport to my city hotel, he told me that he was born in Tehran, in what is now called Iran. Although apologising for his English, he expressed himself clearly and spoke in a quiet way.

Here is my view of his story. It made me think about what he called the 'jungle.'

Beware; it's a jungle out there.
More people want to take than share.
I have seen the good and the bad.
Most of them don't really care.
Why should they, I say?
I'm just a taxi driver.
It's a job and I earn my pay
Helping them on their way.
Yes, for sure, it's a jungle out there.
The game of life is not fair.
There are more losers than winners.

There are few saints and many sinners.
Originally, I come from Persia.
Now, I hear you ask where?
That is the old name for Iran.
I was born in the city of Tehran.
For centuries, we lived in fear.
War after war were frequent there.
That is why I moved away,
Searching for a better day.
So, I went to Germany.
Starting again in poverty.
Learning that life is not easy.
An outsider in a big city.
Yes, beware it's a jungle out there.
Lions and tigers are on the loose.
Watch for the snakes on the street.
Do your talking with your feet.
In the jungle you win or lose.
So, learn quick or surely you'll lose.
Oh, don't be fooled by what you see.
You won't go far without money.
So, prepare, prepare.
Be aware, be very aware.
Life for most is not fair.
Yes, beware; it's a jungle out there.

Questions

What are the main features of the 'jungle' in which you live?

What can you do to improve your chances of surviving and succeeding?

The Priest

Overview

As the sun began to decline on a summers evening, I arrived in a small French village. In the market square, the people were listening to music. The children enjoyed the local fairground, as it was a national holiday.

Nearby, there was a church and I entered to see if I could gain some information on its history. There was no one there, except for the priest. He was busy and we did not speak. He was in his fifties. He looked towards me and I wondered how he felt about his life and work.

Outside in the sunshine, the music and festivities continued. I went to a local bistro and started writing what I thought the priest might have said if we had talked.

I have been a member of the Catholic Church all of my life.
I was born into a Catholic family.
I went to a Catholic school.
I was impressed by the priests and His Holiness.
The laws of the Almighty became my guide.
So, I have dedicated my life to the Catholic Church.
I have had no other work than that of a priest.
My vocation has determined my relationships.
I have never taken a girl out for a walk.
I have no family other than my parishioners.
Each Sunday, I give the sermon in our village church.

But, I no longer believe,
Neither do most of the local community.
They have voted with their feet and are absent.
They worship this world, not the next one.
At the age of 53, I give comfort to the old,
I baptise the new-born,
I marry those who promise often more than they honour.
I bury the dead.
I live alone,
Isolated apart from the institution of the Church
That is increasingly isolated from real life.
My services are increasingly not required.
Marriages are on the decline.
Baptisms are therefore reduced.
Only the funerals keep me busy.
Doctors, nurses, and modern science make even that work irregular.
Fewer priests join the Church.
Those that do are suspected of peculiarities.
We are no longer above suspicion.
And my suspicions grow day by day
For my beliefs have changed.
But, what options do I have now?
Should I share my doubts with my parishioners?
Should I tell the Bishop?
Should I tell His Holiness?
What should I say to the Almighty?

Questions

Are you in a work role that is meaningful in terms of your beliefs and interests?

If not, what do you intend to do about it?

Work

Overview

Maybe I need work more than it needs me? Maybe the work that I do reflects the real me? It helps me make sense of all the nonsense in the world around me. So, I have invented work that helps me to lead and develop an interesting life. Wherever I go on my travels, I look for monuments and stories about amazing people. What I discover is fascinating and provides a great way of meeting new people.

I have also invented imaginary characters in a place called Imagineland, where I write about *Izzy Wizzy*, *Roley Poley*, *Silly Billy*, and others, who come alive through music and song. In addition, I have developed a virtual music group called the 'Can Do Kids' band, who tour the world, learning about the people and culture by playing the local music.

Why do I run the way I do?
Crowding more into each crowded day.
Beating targets of my mind.
Racing the clock, beating time.
Why do I work the way I do?
To make a living and enjoy it too.
Can I do both at the same time?
Is that just a figment of my mind?

So, do I need to change my way of life?
To avoid the stress and strife.
Will I be able to pay my way
As I did yesterday?
So, where do I need to be
In order to be free?
And what will I do tomorrow?

Questions

Work consumes most of our time, but do you enjoy it?

What does work mean to you, and what changes would you like to make?

STREETS OF HOPE

Whatever our situation, we hope that there will be a brighter future, not only for ourselves, but for our families. Many who were born into poverty have worked hard in order to create opportunities for themselves and their children, sustained only by the hope that tomorrow will be a better day.

In these stories, we will meet those who have done as we say, 'the hard yards'. Some of them were victims of war and political persecution. Some of them were born 'on the wrong side of the tracks'. Some of them made choices, which turned out to be poor judgements that led them into difficulties.

On the happy side, you will meet the optimist in the story called 'When I Am A Millionaire'. In real life, many entrepreneurs who succeeded did so because they believed that one day their hopes would be turned into realities and riches. In contrast, 'Casino Nights' tells the story of a compulsive gambler. Although he has high hopes, the cards of probability are always stacked against him. Although he cannot see it, he is on the loser's road, rather than the winner's.

In the world, there are more poor people than there are rich. They see, on television, the streets that they think are paved with gold and try to move to another country, in the hope of finding a better life. Therefore, there are many stories associated with refugees, which are currently being written. The story called 'The Refugee' reflects those who have become victims of war, and search for new opportunities.

All of these stories are about people who hope that tomorrow will bring happiness as well as riches. But, how different are we to them, for we all have high hopes? Can we convert our ideas and aspirations, through hard work and determination, into a satisfying life?

Beggar Or Boss?

Overview

What is it like to grow up in a poor family where one or both of your parents die before you are a teenager?

In South Africa, I met a young boy who asked me for some money. This is my memory of our meeting.

'Do you have any money to help me?' he asked, in a respectful way.
'One minute, I want to take a photo,' I said.
Hout Bay, near Cape Town, South Africa, is a beautiful location.
After taking some scenery shots, I went over to the young boy.
Rather than just give money, I asked him to do a job.
'Would you take my photo?' I asked him.
'Yes,' he said, and I gave him my precious iPhone.
He could have run away with it.
But, there was something about his manner that made me trust him.
He took the photo.
Then, he asked me to move to a different position.
Clearly, he had an eye for a good photograph.
After taking several photos, he walked towards me.
Smiling broadly, he asked me to look at the photos.
Dressed in casual clothes, he looked fit and well.
I asked myself, 'Why was he begging?'

'Do you go to school?' I asked.
'Yes sir.'
He spoke perfect English,
Also, Afrikaans and probably his native tribal language.
'How old are you?' I enquired.
'12 years of age,' he replied.
'Where do you live?' I asked.
'With my grandmother.'
He did not mention the rest of his family.
Does he have brothers and sisters?
Do they all depend on him to bring home some money?
Indeed, what kind of home is it?
Despite his problems, he smiled.
'And where are your parents?' I ask.
'My father lives away from here,' he said, pointing to the shanty town.
'And your mother?'
'She has passed away,' he said with a look of resignation.
'Very sorry to hear that,' I replied, feeling sad.
So, I began to understand why he was begging.
But, he did not act like a beggar.
No, he looked me in the eye and spoke with a quiet confidence.
'So, you live with your grandmother?'
'Yes, but she is not well.'
'What do you do with the money you get?' I asked.
'I buy food and medicine for my grandmother,' he replied.
This was no ordinary beggar.
He had a cause.
'What else do you do to gain money?' I asked.
'If possible, some gardening and car washing,' he answered.
Here was a boy talking like a man:
No self-pity,
No apologies.
I reached for my wallet.
'Thank you for taking my photo,' I said.
'Please accept this for your help.'
'Also, this is for your Grandmother,' I said.
He smiled and said, 'thank you.'
Although, I had little cash, I wished that I had given him more.
'Continue with your education,' I said.
'Yes, boss,' he replied.
I shook his hand.

Again, he smiled.
It was a privilege to have met him.
Had I met a future South African leader?
Was this the next Nelson Mandela?

Question

If you were in a similar situation to this boy, what could you do to improve your chances of having a better life?

Casino Nights

Overview

I live near a casino and also have a friend who has worked in a casino for over 16 years. He has related many interesting and incredible experiences of what gambling does to people, and what people do in order to continue gambling. Maybe that is where I got the original idea for this story. It does not relate to anyone specific. It is purely an imaginary tale, which could be the basis for an exciting film.

I thought I would settle down.
Live the quiet life.
No more nights out on the town.
Make my lover my wife.

Then I thought again, don't give in.
Spin the wheel of chance.
Throw the dice, I can't live twice.
Give me casino nights.

Casino nights, that's where I belong.
Casino nights, a whale of a time.
Casino nights, that's where I shine.
Casino nights, that's right.
Give me Casino nights.

I'm not ready to leave the ring.
Double or quits, one last fling.
Let me see those bright lights.
Give me casino nights.

Casino nights, wine, women and song.
Casino nights, that's where I belong.
Casino nights, black jack and baccarat.
Casino nights, I'm changing my star.
Casino nights, that's right.

Yes, spin the wheel, one more time.
Deal the ups and the downs.
Win or lose, let me choose.
Before I join the clowns.
Casino nights, casino nights.

Questions

What words, in your view, describe the character in this story?

What is your approach to gambling and how would you define it in terms
of your own activity?

Hopes And Fears

Overview

Do you live your life based on an optimistic or a pessimistic approach? Both can be useful depending on the decisions that you make. The result will influence your wellbeing and quality of life. This is now a major area of focus, especially in schools. Teachers are encouraged to help students develop their personal strengths, and to understand how to meet difficult challenges in life. It is also more widely recognised that adults of all ages need to overcome problems and deal with anxieties.

This story reflects important issues that we all have to address.

'What do you do?' I asked.
'Mental Magic,' he said.
It sounded intriguing.
'Explore ways to have a better life, is what I do,' he continued.
'Is your glass half full or half empty?' he asked.
'What do you mean?'
'Well, do you perceive the positive or the negative?
Are things getting worse or better?
Hopes and fears,
Smiles and tears,
That's what life is about,' he said with a smile.
'What is your approach?' he asked.
'Fear the worse and hope for the best,' I replied.
'What evidence do you gain to reduce your fears?' he asked.

'I go to the doctor to get health check-ups,' I replied.
'Also, I get financial statements from my bank.
Every year, I go to my dentist for an assessment.'
'Three sensible things to do,' he responded.
'But, what supports your hopes?'
Do you live in a world of dark or light?' he asked.
'A theatre of sadness or laughter? '
'I am an optimist,' I replied.
'Optimism needs to be supported by substance,' he responded.
'I invent the future and make it happen,' I said in a bold way.
'Those who see the world as positive may be gullible,' he said.
'Those who see the negatives may be more risk averse.'
'They will make fewer mistakes,' he said, looking serious.
'But, they may miss out on opportunities,' I replied.
'Yes, but what is best?
'Running toward is hope,
Running away is fear.
Perception is one thing.
Behaviour is what counts.
So, plan with hope and manage with fear.'
He turned and walked away.

Questions

What are your fears and how will you manage them?

What are your hopes and how will you achieve them?

I'm A Refugee

Overview

Today, there are more and more people migrating, many as refugees, from war and poverty. Some of these are people who just want a better standard of life and move from poor areas to places where they have more opportunities. Refugees may also flee from one area to another, to avoid political persecution. Increasingly, people become refugees because of war. This story reflects how I see one of these people.

I'm a refugee from poverty,
Facing war and death each day.
Struggling and surviving
To try and find a way.
To live my life, like you do
With my family.
To live my life in freedom,
Free of poverty.
Yes, I'm a refugee from poverty.
I see life and death each day
With family and friends of mine
Who couldn't pay their way.
We fight the tide of terror.
The darkness of the storm.
To survive the hell of living

And welcome the new born.
So, join the fight and give your time
To help us in our need.
With your help we can win.
Yes, we will succeed.
I'm a refugee as you can see,
With some rags upon my back,
No money and no food,
Living in a cardboard shack.
I'm a refugee, but don't pity me.
Although, I plead to you.
I'm a pawn in the game
Without a name
And, you are in it too.

Question

What do you think it means to be a refugee?

Silent Children

Overview

Our future depends on our children. But, how can we guide them in a fast-changing world? This is a challenge for parents and teachers, as new technology changes the way we learn and live. For example, what education do people need for the jobs of tomorrow?

The speed of change can cause anxieties in students, who are always under pressure to learn quickly. Some students have the advantage of high levels of care. But, what about those in poor countries, or students in well-developed countries who do not receive requisite support? I share my thoughts in this story.

Silent children walking through
Silver threads of morning dew,
Wondering where they're going to
Tomorrow.

Angel faces smiling bright
Looking outward for a light,
Want to know where they'll be
Tomorrow.

In morning haze the children gaze
Searching daily for the sun.
Questions posed, no one knows
Tomorrow.

Infant creatures, lovely features,
Trusting others, sisters, brothers.
Everyone wanting fun
Tomorrow.

They're our future.
Guide them on their way.
Help them, oh help them
Today.

Questions

What do you think will be the key issues that a child, born today, will have to face when they leave school?

What can we do to help students of today to prepare for tomorrow?

Today's Child

Overview

We see photographs in newspapers and on television of people around the world who are in need. War and famine take their toll. In addition, mismanagement of resources and waste add to the problems in so many poor countries.

This contrasts with the opportunities that children have in western countries, where many feel deprived if they do not have the latest mobile phone or device to connect to the internet. This story brings home the reality - that we all depend on the children of today for our tomorrow.

Your personal wishes, for instant riches.
A silver stake for you to take.
A lottery in the sand.
A blessing or a Witches curse.

A treasure trove, goblets of gold
From sunken mariners of old.
Diamonds dripping, falsely glistening,
A feast of riches beyond the want of need.

And then a face, a small human face.
A child without a meal.
No water, no home, no family.
The reality of life beyond the pale.
What can be done?
A helping hand, a meal, a drink.

Who knows what you can achieve
To rescue a child, if you so believe.

For today's child is our tomorrow.
When we're too old to work, and fend
We will look out into the darkness and hope
That in our need, a helping hand they will lend.

Questions

What can you do to help a child have a better life?

To improve character and self-understanding, what should be taught in schools?

Ubuntu

Overview

The word Ubuntu comes from South Africa. I was told it means, 'I am because you are.' I felt the words, although simple, were powerful, as none of us can exist without the love, help and support of others. We all need to develop the skills of making and maintaining friends, especially when people move around so often. Here are my thoughts.

Ubuntu, Ubuntu.
For you are me and I am you.
Ubuntu, Ubuntu.
There is no place without you.
Ubuntu, Ubuntu.
I am because of you.
You bring the sun, you bring me life.
You are me and I am you.
Ubuntu, Ubuntu.
Oh, what would I be without you?
Ubuntu, Ubuntu.
We are one when we talk.
We are one when we walk.
Ubuntu, Ubuntu.
Yes, I am because we are.

Ubuntu, Ubuntu.
With you always, near or far.
Ubuntu, Ubuntu.
I want you to know that wherever you go
I will be with you, Ubuntu.
And you will be with me, Ubuntu.
Wild spirits running free.
Ubuntu, Ubuntu.
Through the thunder and rain we'll be one.
And when the sun shines again our spirits will run.
Ubuntu, Ubuntu, I love you.
Yes, I love you.
Ubuntu, Ubuntu.

Questions

Who are the most important people in your life?

Have you told them why you feel the way you do, and what they mean to you?

When I Am A Millionaire

Overview

Coming from a relatively poor family, I dreamt of becoming a millionaire and was fortunate to succeed. However, money cannot buy happiness. Relationships are the way to achieve that. This story reflects on what you could do if you are a millionaire and have a good relationship.

When I am a millionaire
With lots of time and money to spare
I'll spend it all on you.

Oh we'll dine at the Ritz and live in Park Lane,
Party till three and dance in the rain,
Holiday in Rio and lie on the beach,
Have a condo in Paris, if we wish.

We'll live in the city and the country, too.
Meeting our friends we'll never be blue.
We'll buy what we want and go anywhere.
Sparkle and shine everywhere.

We'll follow the sun with the jet set.
Meet at the races and put on a bet.
We'll surf in Hawaii and ski in Zermatt.
Living in style, just think of that.
We'll sip champagne and eat caviar,
Gliding past in our Jaguar.

We'll sail the seas and live on my yacht.
Stopping in countries where it's hot.

That's five star living.
Five star play.
Five star loving every day.

We'll visit the Vatican and Venice too.
See Michelangelo, what a view.
Then to Moscow and Tokyo.
Next the Taj and Kathmandu.

Yes, we'll see all the sights on our way.
Then return via the USA.
Because when I am a millionaire
We'll travel first class everywhere.

Yes, when I am a millionaire
With lots of time and money to spare
I'll spend it all on you.

Questions

Who should benefit from the money that you generate, and how?

What are the important causes that you feel should be supported by millionaires?

STREETS OF POWER AND FEAR

In our lives, we all come across situations that can be dangerous. On some occasions, we may fall and have an accident. From time to time, we may become ill and feel that our life is in danger. In times of political unrest, we may feel that violence threatens us. This has certainly been the case for those who have lived in countries where matters of conflict are settled more by the gun than the courts.

In these stories, we will meet those who have experienced danger in their lives and have to find ways and means of overcoming it. One story which reflects the facts of history, but based on my own interpretation, is called 'The Messenger', who warns people of danger, but they ignore him. Other stories give the views from those who were in positions of power, but were not able to use it in order to save themselves.

We all want to avoid the Streets Of Fear. Many seek the Streets Of Power, in order to do so. Some do this by joining the police. Others do it by joining the military. Some people try to resolve their own concerns by becoming politicians. Of course, many people who take on religious roles, such as priests, believe that the power of prayer will overcome fear. You will meet many of these people on your road of life, and these stories will give you insights into the way people think.

Godfather

Overview

Some people become powerful, even though they are not elected or appointed to a formal position. They create their own role by defining the reality and establishing the rules of the relationship.

The term Godfather is usually associated with the Mafia and other powerful gangs. However, it can also apply to those who, over a period of time, gain the respect of others, for what they have done and can do. Here is my view of one Godfather.

Talk is cheap.
Actions speak louder than words.
That is why politicians are not liked:
Too many promises, and too little delivery.
I am not liked by many, but I am respected.
That comes from power.
People around here know that I will protect them.
They can sleep easy at night.
They will not have thieves stealing their prized possessions.
They know I will make their enemies return everything and more.
Yes, people respect me.
I do not have to ask for their votes at an election.
They pay me to keep the peace.
My clients do not trust the police.
Even when the criminals are caught little is done.
There are no guarantees of justice in the law courts.
The only people who win are the rich lawyers.
What a rip off!
Ordinary people can't afford the legal fees.

With me, and my soldiers, they are guaranteed a result.
We have methods that are well tried and tested.
We deliver and don't take prisoners.
That is why I am respected.
Fear is a great motivator.
Those who do not get the message receive something far worse.
My only interest is protecting those who support me.
Money makes the world go around.
It also buys weapons.
I only use them when opponents refuse my generous offers.
Yes, I believe negotiation is the way to solve problems.
If people do not accept my terms, why should I be reasonable?
You ask, where do I get the money?
I have many business interests.
Firstly, there is the insurance business.
People want stability, security and safety.
Of course, it is expensive to provide a 365-day total service.
Next, I am in the relaxation business.
Drugs are part of the equation
But, I don't force people to take them.
They pay me because I provide a service.
I am also in the relationships business.
Nightclubs, where people can drink and gamble, will always make money.
Prostitution can also be profitable, but not where it is legalised.
The rest is trade in various forms.
Shopkeepers and business people pay us to be security guards.
Also, we use our wits and computers to generate money.
We adapt and move with the times.
That is the way to survive.
I keep things simple based on a few key principles.
In this world there is no justice.
There is only power.
If you want me to help you at any time then please let me know.

Questions

Who do you know who is a Godfather figure?

How do they play the role and what results have you seen?

Legless Jimmy

Overview

When I was growing up, the term 'Legless Jimmy' referred to a person suffering from alcohol addiction. This story reflects the sadness and challenges faced by an alcoholic, and the ways it impacts their family and friends.

There are other forms of addiction due to the supply of drugs. In addition, children can become addicted to eating very high calorie food, and become obese. Some people become addicted to playing games and others to gambling. Therefore, the problems of addiction are an increasing concern.

What can you do to ensure you do not become addicted in some way?

Legless Jimmy is a trouble to his friends.
For he likes his drink, on which his money he spends.
Like a sailor on the town, living it up till he falls down.

Legless Jimmy is a burden to his wife
Wasting their money and shortening her life.
He left her homeless through his drinking ways.
Now she prays for better days.
It's the magic in the bottle

And the tragic tricks it plays
That keeps poor Jimmy legless
And wastes away his days.

Legless Jimmy is a terror to his kids
Always fighting and losing his wits.
Wasting his time, drinking all the day
They try to find him and take him away.
But, Legless Jimmy is a mystery to himself.
Always drinking and ruining his health.
Legless Jimmy is a shame to see.
Hope it never happens to you or me.

Oh, why does he do it?
Oh, why, oh, why?
Why does he do it?
I hear you cry.
For, he doesn't know how to change his ways.
So, it ruins all his days.
He can't leave the magic in the bottle
And the tragic tricks it plays.

Questions

What are some of the strategies that can be used in helping an alcoholic?

In what ways can you contribute to helping people in need?

Let's Make The News

Overview

News is increasingly mixed with entertainment. At times, it may be hard to tell the difference.

This story, originally written as a lyric for a song that has been recorded, outlines the choices that have to be made each day by those who present the news. Each of the decisions represent a perception of what is important in the eyes of the newsmakers. But, what is the reality?

Each of us should be the editor of the news of our own life and the way we present it to our family, colleagues and friends. Will it be good news or bad news?

We ask the questions, the stories to make.
Tell us the answers, before it's too late.
Yes, news must be made, regardless of time
For the Editor to give us a by-line.
Oh, we are the media, defenders of truth.
Seeking sensations for the news.
Yes, we are the media, the fifth estate.
Breaking the story, before it's too late.
So, let's make the news, let's make the news.
Tell me what's happening, and I'll give you my views.
Let's make the news, and cover the issues.
I'll tell you what's happening, if you give me your views.
We make the tabloids, the press and TV.
Finding the truth, for you and for me.
But, who's to know what we suppress.
If it's not spicy enough for success.
We are the media, defenders of truth.
Seeking sensations for the news.
To raise the ratings on which we depend.
Should adverts we pursue or freedom defend?
So, let's make the news, let's make the news.
Tell me what's happening, and I'll give you my views.
Let's make the news, and cover the issues.
I'll tell you what's happening, if you give me your views.

Questions

To what extent are you involved in reading the news or making the news?

Do you want to be involved in political action to change the news?

Ravens

Overview

Loyalty, respect, honesty and integrity, form the foundations of trust. But, who can you trust?

Life experience provides the basis for real understanding, but it can be costly in terms of money, time and relationships. Perhaps it would be better if we had clearer ways of assessing how we can trust people.

Ravens ravage the entrails
Picking over the last pieces of the carcass.
Vultures have fed well.
But, how has this come to pass?
Thieves have had their day
Setting upon the unsuspecting,
Presenting themselves with smiles as friends,
Hiding their fangs till darkness descended.
Now, they feast on the remains.
Another good person taken by the wolves.
Hear them howling with delight.
Laughing like hyenas at those who gave them their fortune.
Beware!
That is a sound I know well.

Questions

Who has tried to destroy your way of life?

What have you done to maintain your life when others have attacked you?

No Guarantees

Overview

The question of whether or not our destiny lies in our own hands has been much debated.

Incidents, like the collision of a cruise liner with a large tanker in the North Sea[1], as reflected in this story, provide an example of how our experiences are part of a larger theatre of life, over which we have little control.

Plans made, dates set.
Itinerary charted.
Systems in place.
The illusion of order
Beyond the reality.
The nightmare crash.
Goliaths of the sea
Like warships of old.
Jousting in the dark.
Paint and cyanide ignited.

---

[1] *Following the collision of the 'Norwegian Dream', with a large tanker, in the North Sea. It was the day before we were to board the cruise liner for a holiday - 26th August 1999.*

Sparked by sailing mistakes.
Two thousand souls ask why?
Clear night in radar sight.
Rules and regulations
Defeated by human error.

Question

How much control do you think you have over your own life?

Not Guilty

Overview

I was in a city centre one evening. People were having a good time all around me. Suddenly, an argument broke out which changed the situation.

Violence in public places impacts all those present. What should be done to punish those who instigate the fighting? The judges in the courts often give very short or suspended sentences. This story illustrates one example.

It was a night brawl, that is all.
Another downtown showdown.
Another call to keep the peace.
But, what do they say in court?

'Not guilty, it wasn't my fault.'
'You shouldn't have got in my way.'
'My lawyer says we'll beat the rap.'
'Not guilty - give me justice.'

It was a bright night, violent fight.
Emergency, emergency!
Police on call, a quick response.
But, what do they say in court?

'Not guilty, it wasn't my fault.'
'You shouldn't have got in my way.'
'My lawyer says we'll beat the rap.'
'Not guilty - give me justice!'

So, change the system, defend the victim.
Let the punishment fit the crime.
So, change the system, defend the victim.
Let the punishment fit the crime.
Who is guilty, who is guilty?

Question

Do you believe we get justice from the courts?

Politician

Overview

Every few years, we vote to appoint our political leaders. It is the foundation of democracy and the cherished liberty of free speech. But, do the voters believe what politicians say? The low turnout at most election campaigns suggests that the majority of people no longer believe their vote will make much difference.

To reflect what I perceived as the doubts of many people, I wrote the lyrics for a song and set it to music.

You said you'd make a difference
If we would vote for you.
So, we've given you our confidence
And expect you'll see it through.
These times of trouble, these times of change,
These times of hope, these times of rage
Are with us now for all to see.
Give us peace and we'll all be free.

So, now you've made the big time,
A star on central stage.
Your chance to light the darkness.
To make some useful change.
To help the poor and needy.
To give us a guiding hand.
To listen to those who need you.
To go on and make a stand.

So, make the laws fair for all
And our battles, fight.
Keep prices low and wages high
And we'll be all right.

So, use your power carefully
While you're on centre stage.
It's a place to light the darkness
And make important change.
To feed the poor, to help the sick,
To house the homeless ones.
To fight the crime, to fund the jobs
And to solve a thousand wrongs.

So, make the laws fair for all
And, our battles fight.
Keep prices low and wages high.
And, then we'll be all right.
Oh, yes, we'll be all right.

Question

If you were in a position of power and were are able to make political changes, what would they be, and why?

Secrets Of State

Overview

The Cold War, where secrets are exchanged for money and favours, is an ongoing part of international relations. Major countries spend millions trying to find out if there are nuclear and biological weapons, or technology secrets, that can be gained. However, who holds these secrets and where are they stored?

One day, an elderly man knocked on the door of the US Embassy in Riga, Latvia and said that he had some secrets. He was turned away for not being credible. Scared, in case he was caught, he knocked on the door of the British Embassy. They asked questions and discovered that he could have every possible secret about Russian spies, that they could possibly ever have dreamed of. He was a librarian with access to special information. He held the secrets of both Russian and American spies. His name was Vasili Mitrokhin, the chief librarian of the Russian Secret KGB Service. This story reflects my perceptions of the secret world of spies.

Tinker, tailor, soldier, sailor, spy,
Invisible to the naked eye,
Trained to fit in by being a 'mole',
Professing normality playing a role.
They are the hidden army in our midst,
Searching for secrets at great risk,
Masquerading, lying, waiting their chance.
Work, play or seductive romance.
Dirty tricks, sex, drugs.

Dead of night, fairies or thugs.
But, not Mitrokhin.
Straight face by daylight.
Archiving secrets of the deadly game.
Spiriting them to a hall of fame
For the good of the cause, or personal gain.
The trusted one who knew the tricks.
Why did he do it, why take the risk?
No spy at all, the keeper of the vault.
No suspicion, no search, above fault.
The one who knew all the secret decisions.
So, instead of sending spying missions
We should have asked the librarian.
He would have let us in
Because he wanted out.
Yes, he came knocking on our door
With secrets stolen from the KGB.
His passport to be free.
For the librarian, Mitrokhin, it was a win.
His employers said it was a sin.
But, in the world of spies
Everyone tells lies.

Questions

What are the main ways in which one country spies upon another?

To what extent is spying justified?

The Messenger

Overview

During 1995, there was an enormous earthquake close to the city of Kobe, in Japan. It brought terror and destruction. Over 6400 people were killed and many thousands injured. More than 300,000 people were made homeless. In all, over 400,000 buildings were destroyed.

A few days before, as if by intuition, I wrote a story about a messenger. He gave a dire warning. But, who would listen to a stranger?

His life was written on his face
Stressed and strained, lost in space,
Searching to find a place of peace.
Unshaven, his clothes in tatters, he said,
'I've seen trouble up ahead.
I've made it here to warn you.'
But, few believed what he said.
Nor was he offered food or bed.
Though dressed like a beggar, he did not beg.
He spoke in riddles, roundabout,
Not answering questions,
Spreading doubt.
'Save yourself, leave this place.

Pray for others, ask for grace.
Make peace, face to face.
Beware the terror of the night.
Help those in need.
Then take flight.'
But where to, he did not say.
Nor why they should believe him.
So they said, 'Go away!'
On the road, he went again.
Into the rain, his word to take.
'That soon, near here, the earth will quake.'

Questions

We all receive messages. Which ones do you think are most important for you, at the moment, to allow you to make the right choices for your future?

What part, if any, does intuition play in your decision making?

The Quarry

Overview

I was born in September 1940, as bombs fell all around. The German Nazi leaders sent their Luftwaffe bombers to destroy the ports of Liverpool and Birkenhead. My family lived close by these cities. This story captures my memories of the events, that have had a major influence in my life.

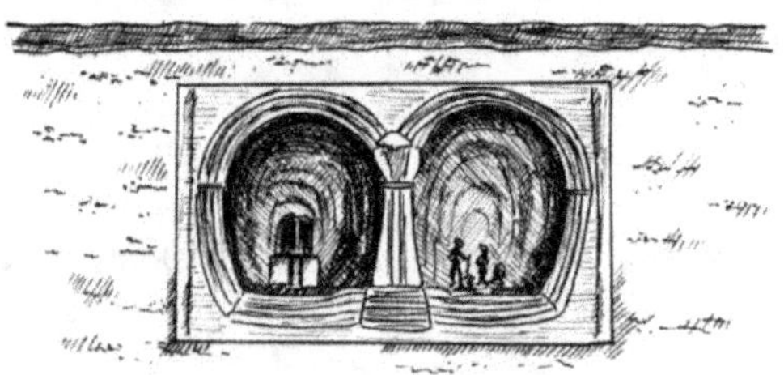

What should we do?
That was the question each night in September 1940.
As soon as darkness fell, danger would be all around.
The Nazi bombers.
Heavily laden planes that had taken off from Germany.
Seeking to destroy Liverpool docks and industry.
'Doodlebugs,' as they were called.
Missing more often than not, and hitting homes and people.
Screeching through the air as they hurtled to ground.
Killing thousands.
Destroying electricity and water supplies.
Wrecking civilised life.
Creating chaos and devastation.
The bombers then turning and returning for more.
Where could women and children run?
'Let's go to the quarry,' my mother said.
'There are caves where we can hide.'
I was still in my first year of life.
Struggling to get a foothold in this mad world.
My mother met with the other mothers.
'What should we take?'
Overnight rugs, some sandwiches and drinks.

Something to lie on.
Sounds like the fare for a picnic.
But, not at midnight.
'How can we look after and feed the children?'
No facilities for toilets or running water.
No cups of tea.
The sound of the air raid siren sounded.
The caves were the only safe place to survive.
Cold and damp, but safe.
Perhaps an illusion, for there was rats.
By oneself it would have been a horror.
With others, there was a sense of camaraderie.
One subject of conversation.
Survival!
Some jokes to stem the anxiety.
Some harsh words of conflict, later regretted.
Essential to stay together.
Not let the enemy divide the group.
Vital that each person supports each other.
Vital to protect the children.
Tomorrow's generation, today's gift.
Living in conditions that were a return to the dark ages.
Waiting for the morning light.
Another day to fight.
Another day to survive.
Another night in the caves.

Questions

Have you had experiences where your life was in danger?

What are your memories from this?

STREETS OF IMAGINATION AND MYSTERY

We all enjoy an entertaining film that takes us into a world of imagination. Likewise, there are many books written which conjure up tales, particularly those of science fiction, which deal with ideas which could come true tomorrow. In the main, we find plays and stories which we often call thrillers, such as those written by Agatha Christie, and other crime writers, engaging and entertaining.

In these stories, you will find examples of both fiction and reality. Indeed, it is said that stories of fact can often be more incredible than those of fiction. For example, think of a time in your own life when a mystery became a reality. Conversations often give clues, which if followed up, can explain mysteries. One of these is the story called 'Skeletons In The Cupboard'. That is a phrase which one of my family members gave to me, and later I found that there was more than an element of truth behind the original conversation, albeit, it was a positive and useful outcome.

Look, therefore, at how you can take the ideas that you come across and convert them into applications, which will be of benefit. One of the greatest examples is how Walt Disney converted his idea about Mickey Mouse into a worldwide business, based upon imagination and mystery, that entertains children and adults. Imagination and mystery are, for some people, escapism. For other people, they are the source of major business ideas, for example, how George Lucas created Star Wars, or how JK Rowling developed the Harry Potter series. Therefore, what are your Stories Of Imagination And Mystery, and what will you do with them?

Beside The Marshes

Overview

There is a restaurant, down a winding road, that leads to the River Dee in England. From across the water I could see the lights of North Wales glinting like stars in the night. To the west, the Irish Sea battered against the coast. In the old days, this is where the sailors came to smuggle their goods from one country to another. This story reflects how it could have happened.

Boats beached high beneath the burning sun.
Smugglers waiting for night to come.
Sailors drinking tots of rum
Beside the marshes.

Coves beneath the mountains
Hiding the secrets of years gone by.
A whiny wind whistles a mournful cry
Beside the marshes.

Secret drinkers of the night
See the signals made by light.

Smugglers running out of sight
Beside the marshes.

Thin trees waving in the breeze.
Old yachts listing at their ease.
Treasure arriving from the seas
Beside the marshes.

Question

How do you think that smuggling has changed from the days of sailing ships to today's use of aeroplanes?

Dreamtime Traveller

Overview

We all escape from reality from time to time, by watching a television series or going to see a film. In doing so, we become involved with someone else's story. The ones that are usually more powerful are those that relate to your own life. Here is an example.

'Follow me,' he said, 'and you will find the answer.'
'To what?' I asked.
'The Truth,' he replied, waving his arms like a conductor of an orchestra.
Dressed in rich robes, he had an air of authority.
Opening the pages of a book, he waved them above his head.
'Read and you will understand,' he cried.
'What will I understand?' I enquired.
'The essence of life and death,' he replied.
He laid a white cloth on the ground.
'Let us pray,' he said.
'I don't believe in prayer,' I replied.
He looked upwards, as if in dismay.
'So, you are a heretic,' he said with contempt.
'No,' I replied, 'I am a psychologist.'

'What religion is that?' he asked.
'It is a profession,' I said.
'I study people's beliefs and behaviours.'
'There is no need,' he shouted.
'There is only one true way to believe.
Our behaviour strictly follows our beliefs,' he shouted with conviction.
'I prefer to have a choice,' I replied.
'The only choice is, are you with us or against us?' he demanded.
'No, there are many options, and we should have freedom of choice,' I said.
Once again he looked to the sky, as clouds covered the sun.
His mood darkened and he pointed his finger at me.
'You are in the Devil's Army,' he shouted.
'No,' I replied in fear, 'I am a tourist seeking explanations.'
'You are a spy for the Devil,' he cried.
'I don't believe in the Devil,' I said.
'You are an enemy of our people,' he exclaimed.
'You cannot be judge and jury,' I protested.
'It is 1492 and I am the Chief Inquisitor of the Spanish Inquisition.
My name is Tomas de Torquemada.
In the name of our Lord, I can do anything I want.'
'Can I have a trial in Court?' I pleaded.
'Torture will be your trial,' he rasped.
'Death by the flames of slow burning, is your sentence,' he screamed.
This time I looked to the sky.
Was there a way of escaping?
So, it was that I awoke, sweating profusely.
Dreamtime travel can be dangerous.

Question

What is the most powerful dream you have had and why?

Family Links

Overview

Ancestry has become both a hobby and a business. But, what secrets lie behind the names and faces in the family album?

With computer aided search facilities, it is relatively easy to trace our family history in terms of names and the dates of birth and death. However, what did our ancestors do with their lives? How has that influenced our own lives?

This story reflects a discovery in my own family history. I know that my great grandmother had a number of children, whose surname was Price. However, there is information to indicate that she had one child whose surname was Margerison. I am a descendent of that person. This story raises questions that I would like to answer.

Something happened along the way.
I wasn't there, I cannot say.
But, no doubt, they had an affair.
Now, would they remember?
Would they care?
To tell me why and where and what?
Or, have they now just forgotten?
For, I would like to go
And, tell my children all I know.

Questions

How far can you trace your ancestry, in terms of where your grandparents and great grandparents lived?

How do you think their lives would have differed to your life today?

Lady In Black

Overview

This is a mystery story. It is based on my thoughts after seeing a well-dressed woman in a hotel. Why was she there? She walked around, as if she needed to be somewhere else. A man appeared and she talked to him. Was this a business meeting, or a liaison?

The words from this story have been used as the lyrics for a song of the same title. It could also be the basis for a film.

In one sense, it is a story of everyday life. But, why did she leave and where was she going?

She was all in black and dressed to kill.
Was she out shopping or seeking a thrill?
For, she had diamonds here and diamonds there
With large sunglasses and long black hair.

She bought a drink and looked around.
Time to think and stake her ground.
She saw her man and gave a smile,
An invitation, full of style.

She could have been his daughter.
She could have been his wife.
She could have been the other woman
Out to change his life.

She could have been the devil.
She could have been a saint.
She could have been so innocent.
A victim of love or hate?

She moved to his table.
And ordered some white wine.
She looked at the menu
As if she were to dine.

Then, she put it in her briefcase.
And casually walked away.
She didn't say a single word,
And, she didn't stop to pay.

She could have been a nice girl
Out and about on the town.
She could have been a foreign spy
Gaining secrets on the sly.

Was she a sinner?
Or, an angel in disguise?
A loser, or a winner?
Spreading truth, or lies?
The Lady in Black.

Questions

We all play various roles at different times. What are the ones that you most enjoy and play well?

How would you write the next segment of this story?

People Who Speak To Us

Overview

Throughout our lives, we are influenced by the ideas and contributions of those around us. Who is it that you need in your life to complement the way you do things? This story illustrates important points that can guide our choices.

We all have photographs that reflect stories from the past, capturing a moment in time, with happy or sad memories. We may also have letters or family records that give us insights into the lives of family and friends. I have tried to keep such family records to pass on to my descendants, so that our lives are remembered and commemorated.

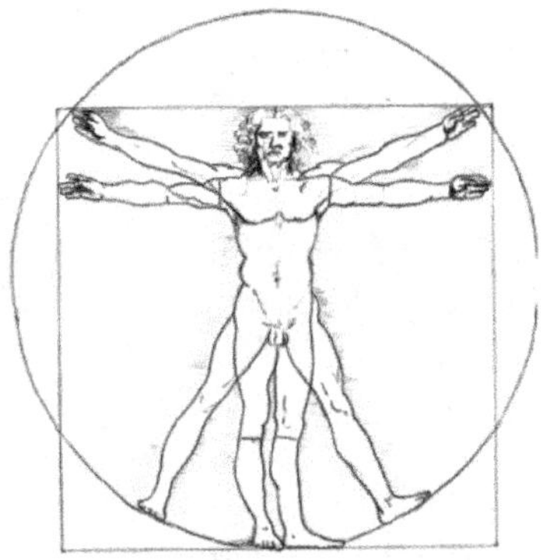

People who speak to us in the still of the night,
Whose magic travels on wings of eternal flight,
Whose talent circles the globe,
Visiting now every home.
People with important things to say.
Speaking today, just like yesterday.
People who often worked alone
Who lived in a world without a phone.
People whose messages still survive.
Touching our heart, changing our lives.
People who did excel
More famous now beyond the bell.
Who are these people we know so well?

That live in a world they could not foretell.
Names that have touched your life.
Poets and philosophers, artists of strife.
Name the names of those who speak.
Were they Roman, were they Greek?
Perhaps Arab, maybe Jew?
Christian, Muslim, or Hindu?
Russian, British or Scandinavian?
Chinese, Japanese, American, Asian?
Prophets, priests and politicians,
Inventors, writers and musicians?
Take the stage.
Now take a bow.
Representatives of yesteryear.
You live again, now.
From the world of words, Shakespeare.
From the world of art, Rembrandt.
From the world of invention, Leonardo.
From the world of music, Tchaikovsky and Mozart.
From the world of religion, Christ and Mohammed.
From the world of sculpture, Michelangelo.
From the world of innovation, Edison.
From the world of science, Einstein.
From the world of medicine, Pasteur and Fleming.
From the world of philosophy, Socrates and Aristotle.
From the world of politics, Churchill and Gandhi.
From the world of engineering, Brunel.
And those whose names were never unfurled
Who gave us the Seven Wonders of the World.
Now, in the new age, who will speak to us today?
And will we recognise what they say?

Questions

Who has inspired you in your life?

How did they influence you?

Personal Secrets

Overview

How easy or hard is it for you to keep a secret? 'Loose lips sink ships,' is an old saying from times of war. But, what secrets do you have today?

Sometimes it is best to listen, rather than to talk. Sometimes it is better to see, but not to say. We are all editors of information. What we say can help or hinder the lives of others.

'What the eye does not see, and the ears do not hear, then the heart does not grieve over,' is another old saying. It is, therefore, worth considering what personal secrets are best kept to ourselves.

We all have secrets, but which ones do we share?
With whom do we confide our inner thoughts?
Friends and maybe enemies of our past?
Concerns and fears that keep us awake.
Never before talked about, never forgotten.
But, some will always last.
Will we share them with those who know us
Wherever they may be?
Secrets locked in the memory of you and me.
Secrets now lost in time and space
Only discussed if we meet face to face.

Secrets with those we have lost from view.
Nor do we know what they do,
Nor where they are and what they say.
May they be careful every day.
Yes, secrets of times past.
Secret memories that will last
So long as we live.
Until then, let us continue as we were.
Carrying the secrets we do not share.

Questions

What secrets should you keep?

How do you decide who you can trust with secrets?

Skeletons In The Cupboard

Overview

In all families, there are stories going back generations. Perhaps, with the passing of time, their origin becomes more mysterious. Maybe the facts become partly fiction.

In my family, we have stories of rags to riches and also riches to rags. There are also stories of marriages that may, or may not, have ever been recognised by either Church or State.

'Skeletons In The Cupboard' was inspired by one of these stories.

Skeletons in the cupboard.
Hear them creak and hear them groan.
Whispering tales of yesteryear
That no one calls their own.
Ghosts that dance at midnight
In cloaks of ghoulish grey,
Whirling in clouds of smoke.
What is it that they say?
Messages with no meaning.
Faces lost in time.
Rushing through the cornfields

To the darkness of the mine.

Skeletons in the cupboard.
Creeping out at night.
Jangling through your mind
Until the morning light.
Mysteries of the darkness.
Searching for the truth.
Burglars on the inside.
Detectives on the roof.
Nightmares by the dozen.
Visions so bizarre.
Tigers on the ice cap.
Moonbeams in a jar.

Skeletons in the cupboard
Rattling your earthly cage.
Once remembered, best forgotten
If you want peace in your old age.

Question

What 'skeletons in the cupboard' do you know exist within your own family and life experiences?

STREETS OF EMPATHY AND REFLECTION

We all reflect on the highs and lows in our lives, and think about what might have been as well as what could be. Such thoughts of reflection help us to learn and plan. The judgements we make determine if our future will be better than our past.

In my meetings with people, I listen to the music of their words. Are the stories they tell sad or happy? Do they express anger or joy? We know from psychological research that emotions can determine not only our quality of life, but the number of years that we live.

Those who develop their skills of empathy, are more able to develop meaningful communication and relationships. Those who can reflect in positive ways, rather than being locked in a web of negative thoughts, are more likely to plan a brighter future. Our lives are determined by such judgements.

In Streets Of Empathy And Reflection, you will meet a lady who had many regrets, who I refer to as 'Virgin Mary'. I also reflect on lessons that apply to all our lives in the story called 'The Thief'. In 'Fly Like A Bird', I explore how we can focus on a positive future, by managing our thoughts. I hope all the stories help you to plan a positive future.

Are You A Winner?

Overview

Many people say they do not like having to make a sale. But, each day, we are judged on our performance. Those who are not seen to make a contribution to the overall sale are left behind.

This story came to me when I reflected on people that I have met in life. Some of them were lying in doorways of shops, and had clearly fallen on hard times. Other people have told me their personal stories of regret. Even though they may have had a good job and money in the bank, they did not feel like winners in their lives.

So, winning is not all about money and power. It is more about one's personal perception. Usually, people have expectations, and they judge if they are a winner in life by the extent to which those expectations are being met.

Did you make a sale today?
Did you win the game?
Striving to keep your job
Have you stayed sane?

Because, I saw an old man fall today
No longer in the race.
No hand to help him on his way.
Defeat upon his face.

Are you a winner
Or, a loser in disguise?
Where are you going?
Tell me no lies.

So, are you going to the city?
Chasing the big sale.
Seeking opportunity
You can't afford to fail.
Are you working and surviving
To make a living wage?
Keeping all your savings
For your old age.

Because, I saw an old man fall today
No longer in the race.
No hand to help him on his way.
Defeat upon his face.

And there, but for the grace,
Go you and me and everyone.
Unless we make the sale.
So help me, as you go on by
To save each other's face.

Are you a winner
Or a loser in disguise?
Where are you going?
Tell me no lies.

Questions

In order to win, where do you focus your energy?

How can you reduce your risks in order to avoid losses?

Choices And Decisions

Life is a series of challenges. Each day there are new choices and roads to be navigated. People often question, with experience and hindsight, whether or not they would make the same decisions again.

This story reflects the hopes and fears we all encounter on life's journey.

If only we could see ahead
The twists and turns on life's road.
Knowing we are going up or down.
Seeking the way to satisfy our inner voices.
In the external world of temptation
Each step a risk.
Our decisions, the difference between success and failure.
Judgement is easier with hindsight.
Reading the wind and the tea leaves.
Charting a course and assessing the risks.
Finding which way to go.
Discussion and discoveries.
Punishment or reward.
Heaven or hell on earth.
Confidence competing with fear.
Yet, we live in hope
To avoid sickness and seek success.
To invest our time for tomorrow
While enjoying today and guarding the gains of yesterday.
Trying to earn enough to live on and more to save

For the rainy day.
Knowing when to stay and play.
Knowing when to run and hide.
Knowing where the comfort zone is.
Yet, not resting on our laurels.
For nothing is forever.
Only faith, judgement and hope.

Questions

What are your hopes?

How can you make them become a reality?

Fly Like A Bird

Overview

Sometimes we get so caught up in living life, with all its demands and ups and downs, that we lose sight of the direction in which we are going.

This story deals with some of these issues.

Are you driven by your demons through the darkness of the maze?
Do you swim for your life against the pounding waves?
Wondering are you dreaming, or on a mystery tour?
Seeing friends dancing near the ocean shore.
Are you a victim of your virtues on the rocky road of life?
Do you crave for peace and happiness instead of all this strife?
Working for a future with no certainty in sight.
Waiting for the morning sun to banish fears of the night.
Are you a slave to the systems created by the wise?
Can you believe what you see, is it a mirage of lies?
Reading without understanding, a time of mystery.
A time beyond compare, an illusion or reality.
Can you read the signs of danger in the shiny stars above?
Can you find on earth a person, who you can truly love?
For living is the journey, as we travel in haste.
Flying by so quickly in this stressful human race.
Are you a follower of fashion, inventions of your mind?
Can you manage situations beyond reason and rhyme?
Is there method in your madness, guiding your decisions?
Happiness or sadness, that lies beyond your visions.

So, ride the road of life, surf the internet.
Fly high like a bird, don't worry what is said.
Yes, fight for your rights, let your voice be heard.
Don't wait till tomorrow, fly like a bird.
Yes, fly, fly high, fly like a bird.

Questions

Do you know where you're going and why?

What are your plans for the next year?

Just Like Me And You

Overview

This is a fun story about a shy person, to whom life, and how it works, is all a bit of a mystery to him.

We are all faced with various challenges in our own lives. It is the choices we make, and how we deal with what life throws at us, that is most important.

A friend of mine was very kind to all the girls he knew.
But, when it came to courting
He didn't have a clue.
We gave him books and videos and lots of pictures too.
Yet, when he came to wooing
He didn't have a clue.
So, we took him to a doctor, who told him a thing or two.
But when he came to use it
He didn't have a clue.
We went to the pub one day and had a drink or two.
He chatted up the barmaid
But she was 72.
So, we sent him to a lady, with experience and tact.
She asked him in, for that's no sin,
And told him all the facts.
Then, she showed him what to do, and the benefits he'd gain.
But, he showed little interest

And, we wondered was he sane?
At last, he met a nice girl, who knew a thing or two.
She led him on and on.
And, he slowly got a clue.
So, at the age of 42, one day, all of a sudden
He married this girl aged 22
And, now they've got six children.
Yes, he's got a mortgage, just like me and you.
But, how is he going to pay his debts?
He hasn't got a clue.
No, he hasn't got a clue blue.
Not a single, bloody clue.
He hasn't got a clue, blue.
He's just like me and you.

Questions

What are you passionate about?

Do you know what direction you would like to take in life?

Raised Hands

Overview

A journey to Germany made me realise how time makes a difference. My father, and his generation, fought for our lives and freedom. Now, we are welcomed as tourists.

How does one generation deal with its inheritance from the other? This applies in families, as well as at a national level. One of my friends said that he and his family had been cursed by their history. In my case, I feel I have been blessed by my family and national history. What do you feel is your situation and what will you do about it?

This reflects my experience on a holiday visit.

What a difference time makes.
Raised hands of recognition.
Smiling faces from the crowd.
Raised hands waving a welcome.
Immigration entry without question.
No military, no guns.
Only the wind and tide oppose us.
Sailing through the Kiel Canal.
Yet hands were raised differently
Within our living memory.
Raised hands of the Nazis,
Marching jackboots with the swastika.
Raised hands for the bayonet strike,
The bombs, the tanks, the smell of death.

Raised hands of resignation
To the holocaust camps of death.
Raised hands of surrender
To the deadly Waffen SS execution squads.
Raised hands of the children
Whose parents perpetrated those atrocities?
Raised hands of welcome.
Who could believe that it is happening here?
Raised hands of freedom.

Question

Do you believe in forgiveness?

See You

Overview

This story is about someone having a hard time. We all rely on our friends and family for support during our lives.

Imagine how hard it must be for those who have no one, whether it is because of situations or circumstances that they have created for themselves, or for reasons outside of their control.

See you kneeling at the Cross
Silently in prayer.
Asking for forgiveness,
Secrets to share.

See you walking empty streets
In the early hours of morn.
Looking for a shelter,
Tired and forlorn.

See you weeping at the graveside,
More heavily than the rain.
Clutching a broken flower,
Whispering a name.

See you turn and walk away
So slowly down the lane.
Holding that broken flower,
Whispering that name.

Who are you?
From where do you come?
Why are you here?
Praying in hope or fear?

Questions

For what, do you think this person is searching?

Do you know anybody in a similar situation and, if so, what can you do to help?

The Thief

Overview

Inside each person there is a time clock that determines how our bodies respond to age. Some people experience the visible effects of ageing, such as for example, those who lose their hair early in life. Others may have symptoms of pain associated with arthritis. Athletes notice that by the time they have reached the age of 30, their speed and consistency of performance has probably reached its peak and is hard to sustain.

Compared to others, I have been fortunate. My body clock has meant a few things have worn out, but brilliant surgeons have given me a high quality of physical life. Also, I have been able to continue my professional work, which demands a high level of creativity and business problem solving.

However, no one is immune, and I reflected on the fact that there is a time thief at work within all our bodies. So, use your time well, while you still can.

Age crept up on me
Like a thief in the night.
Stealing my prized possessions.
Stealthily, in a secret way.
So, I did not see them disappear.

Gradually, I felt things were missing.
I knew more, but remembered less.
My eyes strained to see that which was once clear.
My legs took longer to cover shorter distances.
And the Thief returned at regular intervals
Stealing my energy.

I reported the Thief to my doctor.
He said I was lucky not to have lost more.
He recommended better self-protection.
I therefore now take active steps:
Walking, running, and jumping.
They slow the Thief down, but he will return.

Insurance is no answer, nor prayer.
Only one thing will remain, when everything else is stolen.
The Thief will not steal our Achievements.

Questions

What can you do to protect yourself from 'The Thief'?

How can you increase your achievements?

Virgin Mary

Overview

Some of the most important stories come from what people say when away from home, when they have time to relax and reflect. At a dinner one evening, I sat next to a teacher who talked about her life story. We never met again, but what she said made me think, and I wrote this in her honour.

It is all different now.
In my day, we grew up thinking the end of the world was coming.
They called it the Cold War.
Nuclear weapons could blow us up.
What was the point of marrying and having children?
So, I didn't, but now regret it.
Thought I was doing the right thing at the time.
What was the point of having children caught in another war?
But, now I'm getting older and have no family.
I can't turn the clock back and start again.
There was a time when I thought of adopting a child.
But, I realised it would not be easy.
I felt I would be like the Virgin Mary
Only in my case there was no Joseph,
Never has been.
In my day, there was no sex education.

One night of risk could be a lifetime's punishment
So, I did not bother.
Studied hard and got a teaching job.
Some people say I have never left school.
In one sense they are right.
But, I have taught some interesting students.
No doubt they have seen a lot more of life than myself.
But, could they have done it without me?
As an English teacher to foreign students, I gave them skills.
Many of the boys now drive fast cars.
As for the girls, they live in the fast lane.
Women's liberation is a way of life, not a protest movement.
They have few fears.
The morning after pill solves any problems from the night before.
Career comes before a family.
Enjoying today, and letting tomorrow be what it will be.
Friends become partners.
Living together, but not in marriage.
Or, separating because there are no legal ties,
Which is rather ironic.
For different reasons they may become more like me.
Living with a cat for company.
After all, there is only a limited time.
Or, will they have children by adoption?
Will each one of them become the new Virgin Mary?

Questions

What kind of life do you lead, and is it what you want?

If not, what will you do to change it?

Virtual Memorial

Overview

Understanding more about one's ancestry is becoming more popular. It is a hobby for many, as they develop their family tree. Some people arrange their holidays to visit relatives, and travel around the areas where their ancestors lived.

Today, we can provide our future family with stories, pictures, audios and videos of our lives. So, I have created various documents about my life and that of our family and put them on to the Internet. I hope my grandchildren and their children will appreciate them, and understand what we did with our lives.

Should I wait for them to celebrate my life
Beyond the marks I have made?
Should I wait for them to decide how I will be remembered
Beyond my photographs and videos?
Should I wait for them to choose my memorial
Beyond my writings and my songs?
Should I wait for them to remember me
Beyond my wife, my sons and daughters?
And what should the celebration be
Beyond a statue, a painting and a stone?
And why should it be confined to Earth?

Beyond, there is the World Wide Web.
Yes, there I shall create a multi-media celebration.
A reality defined by what I see.
A virtual reality that is me.

Question

What would you like written on your memorial, for people to remember you?

Yesterday Today

Overview

Photographs capture people, places and points in time. While in Copenhagen, Denmark, I visited a museum. The photographs were all in black and white, reflecting life over 100 years ago. Each image presented a story without words.

This is my interpretation of what those involved were doing[2]. If only the people from those images could come back to life and tell us about who they were and the turns and twists of their own life stories. No doubt, each one would have a tale to tell.

Faces staring from the frame
Living for a second once again.
Though their time has long since gone
Through their picture they live on.

Skaters in silhouette.
Children playing in the wet.
Businessmen on the quayside.
Sailors waiting for the tide.

---

[2] *Based on a photographic exhibition, in an old windmill I visited, in the centre of Copenhagen, Denmark.*

Streets Of Empathy and Reflection

Chimney sweeps, top hats and brooms.
Working girls at their looms.
Ladies cycling three abreast.
Christmas shopping at its best.

Canal boats in deep water slips.
Side by side with larger ships.
Navy girls on shore leave,
Dressed to kill in short weave.

Night descends upon the town.
Worried faces look around.
See the Hun with their goose step.
New rules only fools forget.

War by day and by night.
Living and dying by candlelight.
1945 and liberation.
Flags aloft in jubilation.

Back to work, civilisation
Beyond the camps of concentration.
Boys at play, girls out skating
Beneath the gaze of parents waiting.

A liner sounds a last farewell.
Waving hands, fond messages tell.
A generation of rock and roll,
Marches and protests that stirred the soul.

Searching for a new identity.
Challenging authority.
On the road with CND.
Ban the bomb, but not the nudity.

Smoking pot in public places.
Funny times, private rages.
Building houses for one and all.
Family shopping and football.

Politicians and priests out promoting.
Saints and sinners decide by voting.
Pictures for each and every year.
A smile, a laugh and a tear.

All Denmark in black and white.
A hundred years of changing life.

Questions

What has been the happiest time of your life?

What were you doing at that time, and with whom?

STREETS OF RELATIONSHIPS

Relationships define our lives. The people we meet listen to our stories and share their own. In the process, we make friends and enemies, and increasingly those we call 'frenemies', when in friendly competition. It is through relationships at home, in our work, and in social groups, that we learn with and from others.

In the following stories, I have written about people that I would like to meet, as well as those I have met. Some of the tales could be made into a film. 'Mizzie From Mississippi' is an example. I never met the lady, but would like to have done so. Another story that could be a film is 'Wanted Man', who is in a relationship, but cannot disclose who he is. The same applies to 'A Stranger, My Brother'.

A number of stories could be made into songs, as for example, the one called 'It's Our Time' and 'Where Are You?' All of these stories illustrate different aspects of relationships. If you write about the relationships that you have had, what would be the main themes?

A Stranger, My Brother

Overview

While travelling, we all meet people briefly and then never see them again. Occasionally, someone says something which is important. If we ask the right question, we may find this person has significance in our life. This story is an example of a brief meeting, which turns out to be more than that, as they both have links to each other, previously unknown.

When some people get an idea for a story, they write a book. I usually write a lyric for a song. Sometimes that lyric becomes the basis for a poem, or 'prosoem' as I call them. That is a mixture of prose and poem. This story is an example. It could be the basis for a film or video. Where will it go next? Maybe you would like to write the follow up.

He said he was a singer, looking for his roots,
Trying to find his family.
I told him I was an orphan, born in poverty.
He asked from which city?
'I was born not far from here,' I said.
'Somewhere on the north side, up there.'
'That's funny,' he replied, 'Cos that's where my mother died.

That is why I am here, to see what I can find.'
He said he had a sister, although he'd never seen her.
But, he knew her name was Anna.
I smiled with surprise, and said, 'That's my name too.'
He nodded and said he knew.
'How come you know that?' I asked.
'The guy at the bar told me,' he said, 'that's why I came to talk.'
He said, 'I've got a question, do you mind?
Cos, I know when my sister was born.'
'When was that?' I asked.
'The fourth of July,' he said, 'nineteen seventy eight.'
'You won't believe it,' I said, 'That's my birthday.
And I was born in seventy eight.
Is this too big a chance?
Could it be coincidence?'
'Well,' he said, 'There's one more test before DNA
Cos, my mother gave my brother a double name.
I am called Stefan Johan,' he said.
Cos my dad was European, but called me John.'
'But, that is the name my mother told me about.
Are you my brother, is there a doubt?
Cos, you look like me, you talk like me.
I want to believe you are my family.'
He took my hand and said, 'Here is a picture of our mother.'
And with that, I knew I had found my brother.

Questions

Searching for ancestors in the historical records has become a major hobby as well as big business for organisations.

What are you interested in discovering about the history of your family?

Gods Of Time

Overview

We all live by certain principles and guidelines, which we believe to be helpful in our lives. Some of these derive from religion, as there are many so-called Gods that have emerged from the early days of the Greeks, Romans, and other communities. However, what do we mean when we refer to the 'Gods of Time'?

I met them yesterday.
'Don't delay,' I heard a Time God say.
'Yes, it's time to be on your way,' he stressed.
'The clock is ticking.
Tick, tock, tick tock,
Unbolt the lock.'
'Yes,' said the Time God, time to go.'
'Where to and what to do? I asked.
'That is up to you,' rasped his partner, Ms Goddess.
'Don't wait, or you'll be late, she added.
'Time is impossible to reclaim.'
'So what is your aim?' asked the Time God.
'To have a good time,' I replied with a smile.
'Happiness is better than fame.'
'That is all in the mind,' said the Time God.
'Many things can bring you pleasure.
Even work, as well as leisure.'
'Make time your passion,' said the Goddess.

Don't change with fashion,
Apply your time wisely.
Learn how to spend it carefully.'
'How much time do you spend with your friends and family?' asked the
Time God
'Not enough,' I thought.
'How much time do you give to helping others in need?' asked the Goddess.
Again, there was doubt on my conscience.
'How many minutes are there in a day?' asked the Time God.
'I will have think,' I answered playing for time.
'Twenty four times sixty,' he replied, 'makes 1440 minutes.
'That is how you can start to use your time well.
Time spent thinking about your future is time well spent.'
'Discover your purpose,' added the Goddess.
'Then choose your priorities and make plans.
Allocate your time well.
Measure your inputs by your outputs.
Always convert what you learn.
That will determine what you earn.
It's not the days in your life that decide your fate.
It is the life in your days you need to rate.
There is no going backward.
You can only go forward.
You are what you do.
You will be how you use your time.'

Questions

How well do you feel you use your own time, in order to earn a living, keep fit, and maintain relationships with family and friends?

What do you plan to do in order to improve your use of time? Will it be to spend more time working, on holidays, with friends, or on some other activities that are important to you?

I Like Your Style

Overview

Relationships, personal preferences and choices are all central to our success in life. We are influenced by the ideas and behaviours of those we meet, which can have a big influence on our own approach to life.

Below, is a story of some that I have met on the road of my life.

I'm Mr Anonymous, though not monogamous.
I live by myself, alone.
And, I like it that way, but, not every day.
At nights, I like to roam.
I'm Ms Autonomous, though, it's not synonymous,
Living by myself, alone.
So I go where I want, whenever I want.
And you'll find I'm well known.
Well, I like your style.
And I like your way.
But, you don't have too much to say.
But, that's okay.
I'm always working, but that's not a sin.
Unless you break the law.
And I drive myself hard.
For I'm a wild card.

And what I like, I ask for more.
I'm not easily pleased.
Though I like to be teased.
By someone who knows my ways.
For while objective, I'm quite subjective.
When it comes to play.
Let's give it a go and make our show.
For as long as it suits us best.
Let's stay anonymous and autonomous.
And be each other's guests.

Questions

How would you describe your personality?

What style of life do you want?

It's Our Time

Overview

It is important to find time to give to a relationship, in order for it to develop and blossom.

By sharing our hopes and dreams, as well as the many ups and downs of daily life, with our friends and family, we are better able to negotiate and make sense of our life, and the directions and choices we make.

In our life, we need some time.
Yes, time to dream.
And time to rhyme.
Time without a deadline.
Yes, time for you and me.
Yes, it's our time.
By ourselves, alone.
A quiet time.
No office and no phone.
Yes, it's our time.
A time we have for dreaming.
A time of care and meaning.
A time to call our own.
Yes, it's our time.
Peaceful, all alone.
A treasured time.
A time we have for sharing.

A time of love and caring.
A time to call our own.
So give us space.
Yes, give us time.
When I am yours.
And you are mine.
Oh, let us meet.
In our secret place.
And find ourselves again.

Questions

How do you use your time?

What can you do to improve the use of your time?

Lessons Of Life

Overview

We all have listened to speeches from politicians, priests and professors, as well as family members and friends, which encourage us to make the best of our life. No doubt, these were based on lessons of hard won experiences. What can we learn from the experiences of others?

Here is my version.

As I entered the school hall, the chatter subsided.
The Head Teacher went to the rostrum.
'Today, we will focus on lessons from life,' she said in a sombre way.
As I sat, ready to speak, I realised she meant my life.
I had been invited to speak to the Students' Assembly.
There they were, all shining bright, more conscripts than volunteers.
After a short introduction, the Head Teacher invited me to speak.
Should I start with a joke, a quote or a story?
Although I had made many speeches before, my pulse was racing.
Over 200 young eyes and ears were waiting.
Most important, their young minds would interpret my words.
'Hello,' I said, 'Thank you for inviting me to your Assembly.'
'In this series of presentations, I understand you have heard
from many speakers.
Some talked about their lessons from sport, from work,
and from volunteering.

Instead, I would like to start with a question.
What do you think people who achieved a great deal focused upon?'
I mentioned Shakespeare and Marie Curie.
In addition, I said, 'Mozart and Florence Nightingale were examples.'
Asking the students to work in groups of three, they began to discuss.
A babble of noise erupted from the school hall.
The Head Teacher looked at me in a quizzical way.
'I thought you were going to give them a speech,' she said.
Clearly, I had upset her expectations.
'We've only got 20 minutes before they go to their classes,' she added.
'What I have to say will only take a few minutes,' I replied.
'Do you have any visuals, to show the students?' she asked.
'No, I will ask them to develop their own,' I responded.
The discussions amongst the students were in full swing.
Laughter, in some groups, drowned the buzz of conversation.
After about five minutes, I put up my hands.
It had a magical effect.
'Can you let me know some of the points you discussed?' I asked.
A student put up his hand and I asked for his comments.
'Our group felt that the high achievers worked hard,' he said.
Another student spoke, 'We felt they developed their skills and talents.'
Within a few minutes, many ideas were shared.
I wrote each one on a white board.
When we had a good list of points, I turned to the students.
'I work as a psychologist,' I said.
'In short, that means I study people's attitude and behaviour.
In particular, I focus on helping students and adults make the best of
their lives.'
Turning to the list, I read out the key points the students had suggested.
'This list represents a psychological experiment.
It summarises your views of what is seen as important
for you to succeed.
So, keep a copy and follow your own advice.
As for me, I learnt a lot from others with more experience.
I have studied the lives of over 500 amazing people.
Achievers like Pasteur, Tubman, Edison, Keller and Blackwell.
Great names in science, civics, innovation and medicine.
We can learn how they used their time and made successful judgments.
Also, each day, I meet people with a range of skills and experience.
So, I ask questions that encourage people to share what they know.
In many cases, the questions are more important than the answers.

They show that you respect others and help develop relationships.
Next, the judgments you make will determine your standard and style of life.
So, be wise in how you spend your time.
Choose your friends and the actions you take, carefully.
Learn when to be reactive to situations and when to be proactive.
Above all, create a plan to develop your talents.
Make sure you protect your health and energy.
Although you will learn about subjects at school,
Life is about learning from action,
That means personal and practical psychology.
So, study what you like and dislike, and act accordingly.
Invest in your own self-development.
Everyone is a psychologist of their own experiences.
It is valuable to study the psychology of how to learn and live a happy life.
I wish you well.'

Question

If you were asked to give advice to young people, or a friend, what are the main lessons from your life experience that you would share?

Man Of The Streets

Overview

In our lives, we make many journeys. But, which streets will take us where we want to go? Sometimes, the situation defines our options. But, how do we create situations that will give us satisfaction and happiness in our lives?

This story reflects questions based on my experiences.

I am a man of the streets.
They were the streets of war when I was born.
Nights of thunder from the bombs.
Days of despair from the destruction.
I am a man from the streets of my youth.
A time of hope and 'rock and roll' rebels.
I gained my first job, near the Cavern Club in Liverpool.
Beatles' music and Mersey sounds were all the rage.
Yes, I am a man of many streets.
Learning career skills on the streets of London.
Surviving the concrete jungle.
But, am I street wise?
Some streets are dead ends, leading nowhere.
Some are fast tracks filled with promises.
What street do you wish to follow?

Is it 'Easy Street?'
Or, a street called 'Desire?'
Yes, there are many streets.
Some are straight with a clear view.
Others are full of crazy zigzags with ice.
On your way, you will reach crossroads,
Streets of opportunity, or streets of danger?
You can walk, run, cycle, drive, swim or fly.
But, where will you go?
Speed is no substitute for direction.
What street are you on now?
Is it an uphill climb or a downhill slide?
Is it paved with rocks or gold?
Yes, I am a man of the world's streets.
I have seen slow lanes and fast lanes.
People in poor streets and rich streets.
The lonely streets and the party streets.
Watching the reciprocal deals on 'two-way' streets.
Seeing the power on one-way streets.
Your judgments define who you will become.
Learn when to change direction.
Know when to speed up and when to slow down.
Decide when to advance and when to retreat.
We are all men and women of the streets.
So, be careful which ones you take on your life journey.
We have all made mistakes and taken the wrong turn.
Search for those that suit your style.
Will they be streets of fame and fortune
Or streets of safety and security?
Will you stay in local streets or travel
In search of a better tomorrow?

Questions

What is the name of the street of life that you are on now?

What is the name of the street of life, which you would like to be on in the future, and how will you get there?

Mizzie From Mississippi

Overview

Who have you met on the road of life that has influenced you, both in a positive and negative sense? The people we meet and choose to trust, and the places and roads we travel along, all contribute to our own life journey.

This story is set in New Orleans, in the great days of the jazz clubs. Although, Mizzie, and her relationship with the clarinet player is a figment of my imagination, it illustrates what we can learn from life experiences.

I met him in a jazz bar, on the other side of town,
Playing clarinet with a traditional kind of sound.
I took him at his word and followed him around,
Listening to the blues.
He was handsome, he was charming, totally disarming.
And I fell for him, listening to the blues.
He was 30, going on 40 and yes, he could be naughty,
But, the kind of man I choose.
He asked me for some money, to help him pay a debt
And told me he'd repay me, when he'd had a bet.
I took him at his word and gave him what I had.
But, he blew it, as I listened to the blues.

Oh, he seduced me, he abused me, without doubt, he used me.
When I fell for him, listening to the blues.
He confused me, he bemused me, and totally defused me.
That man was sure bad news.
Yes, I'm Mizzie from Mississippi,
A country girl in town,
Liking a good time,
But, surprised by what I found.
Now, I don't need that man in my life,
Causing me lots of strife.
No, I don't need that man in my life, anymore!

Questions

How would you describe Mizzie's personality?

Have you had to make choices similar to those of the person in the story?

Old Friend

Overview

The friendships we share, throughout our lives, vary. Some are short term, others are for a lifetime, and their impact is significant.

They all need to be celebrated in their own way, as they contribute to how we grow and develop. When you meet old friends, you automatically begin reflecting on the times you shared together.

Her face was thinner than I remember.
But, she still had the same welcoming smile.
The wind rustled through her hair, now shorter and thinner.
She walked more slowly, but determined as ever.
Eager for news and views.
So many questions and things to say.
So little time, in a crowded day.
Interesting to compare our different roads and pathways.
Highways and byways, and some dry gullies.
The highs and lows, now half forgotten.
But, still reminding us of yesterday, and what might have been.
A meeting by chance, not destined for romance.
Not then, nor now, each with so many commitments.
But, good to meet again.

Part of our identity wrapped up in each other's youth.
Our lives changed for the better at that time.
Learning how to live and give, yet not share forever.
We moved on, in different directions.
Choices of the day, decisions of a lifetime.
Now, seeing life for what it is, and giving thanks,
Counting our blessings,
Wondering if they would have been more or less?
Meeting once again, this time with memories.
A smile, a shake of hands, a wave.
What a difference 40 years makes.

Questions

Who are the old friends that you remember?

How have they influenced your life?

The Relationship

Overview

We all need friends. As John Donne famously wrote, 'No man is an island.' Indeed, loneliness is a major problem for both the elderly and the young in modern society, where people can become lost, even though surrounded by millions in major cities.

So, it is interesting to see how people have long lasting relationships. This is a story that is an example, partly based on fact, and partly on fiction. It provides a basis for discussing what makes a long-term successful relationship.

Smiling, he walked toward the bar.
'What would you like?' asked the bartender.
'Company,' he replied.
'We don't sell that,' said the bartender.
'Then, give me a beer.'
Seeing a good-looking girl, he went over.
'Hi, I'm new in town,' he said, with a deep North American accent.
Leaning forward, she asked, 'Where do you come from?'
'Small town in Canada, near the Rocky Mountains,' he replied.
'Why are you here?' she asked.
'Looking for work and friends,' he said, as he took a drink.
'Are you married?' she enquired.
He paused, smiled again and in a drawl said, 'No, not yet,

But, I've been divorced five times.'
She laughed and they talked about their work.
'I am a hair dresser,' she said.
'Maybe I can be a client,' he replied with a big smile.
'Here is my business card and phone number.'
'Got to be going,' he said.
'Where to?' she asked.
'Must find a place to stay,' he said.
'There is a room for rent above my shop,' she indicated.
'Sounds interesting,' he said, 'could I see it?'
'Yes, I'll introduce you.'
So, they walked into the sunshine.
The start of a long journey.

Question

Think of the interesting people you have met on the road of life. How did some of those relationships start?

The Time When I'm With You

Overview

Time can pass slowly, or quickly. It depends on what you are doing and with whom you are talking. Those who are more extroverted in their preferences will enjoy the company of others. Maybe that is why I wrote these lyrics for a song.

It's a special time, a timeless time.
A time in space, close face to face.
The time I love the best.
The time when I'm with you.

It's a time of hope, a time of peace.
It's a time of freedom, a time to please.
The time I love the best:
The time when I'm with you.

Oh, when I'm with you, the stars blaze bright.
I don't fear the darkest night.
I know that I'm alive
When I'm with you.

It's a special time, a timeless time.
Is it a mirage in my mind?
A time beyond compare:
The time when I'm with you.

It's a time of hope, a time of peace.
It's a time of freedom, a time to please.
The time I love the best:
The time when I'm with you.

Oh, when I'm with you, the stars blaze bright.
I don't fear the darkest night.
I know that I'm alive:
When I'm with you.

It's a special time, when time stands still.
Holding hands, high on the hill.
The time I love the best:
The time when I'm with you.

Question

Who are the most important people with whom you enjoy spending time, and why?

Trust In Me

Overview

Every meeting tells a story. Is it for business or pleasure? Is it friendly or fraught with differences of opinion? When writing lyrics for songs these are questions that I ask and try to answer.

This story reflects two people that I observed having dinner. I did not hear what they said, but imagined what was really at stake from their body language.

Brief encounters, small talk time.
Scotch on the rocks, and sweet white wine.
But where's the meaning and common ground?
You show me your feelings, without a sound.

So break the ice, shake the door.
What are we fighting for?
So trust in me and I'll trust in you.
Let's cast aside what has past.

Share a table, one more time.
Dinner in town, and French red wine.
There's new meaning, flowers arrive.
We share our feelings, let's keep them alive.

Yes break the ice, shake the door.
What are we fighting for?
So trust in me, and I'll trust in you.
I will trust in you.

Questions

Who do you need to talk to in the next few days, in order to improve a relationship?

What will you talk about, and why?

Wanted Man

Overview

The essence of all strong stories is the element of mystery. In writing lyrics for songs, I have long been interested in lyrics that have an unknown ending. The story of 'Wanted Man' reflects a person who has a dark and dangerous secret.

In your life, you will have met or will meet someone who is mysterious. How will you find out who they really are?

'Would you like a coffee?'
Were the simple words she said.
And like a wine of a different kind
It went straight to my head.
She filled my cup with a smile
And asked me where I'd been.
I said, I'd been travelling far
And told her what I'd seen.
'For I've seen trouble, I've seen war.
I've seen ghosts, and a whole lot more.'
But, should I tell her who I am?
Should I say, 'I'm a Wanted Man'?
'Would you like to stay a while?'

She asked so quietly.
I gave her a gentle kiss
And accepted gratefully.
The days, they passed quickly by.
And the seasons, they did turn.
We grew to love each other.
With our son and daughter.
'But, I've seen trouble, I've seen war.
I've seen ghosts, and a whole lot more.'
Should I tell her who I am?
Should I say, 'I'm a Wanted Man'?
'Would you like to marry me?'
She asked one summer's day.
And while that's what I wanted.
I had to turn away.
'Cos, I've seen trouble, I've seen war.
I've seen ghosts, and a whole lot more.'
But, should I tell her who I am?
Should I say, 'I'm a Wanted Man'?

Questions

Who is the most mysterious person you have met and why?

What lessons about life did you gain from this story?

Where Are You?

Overview

Travel brings the opportunity to see new places and meet new friends. But, in the process, we leave behind existing friends.

I wrote this story as a lyric for a song that was recorded beautifully by the singer, Calli Hughes, on her album called *Remember Me*.

Another town, another night, another room.
But, it's not right, without you.
Another plane, another flight, another meal.
No candlelight, without you.
Why did you go away?
Oh, what did I say?
Please, tell me, where are you?
Where did you run that day?
Oh, what did I say?
I'm searching, still searching for you.
I'm searching each crowded avenue.
Another phone, unanswered tone.
Another town, and I am down without you.
Another day, what can I say?
Another town, but it is not mine, without you.
Why did you go away?
Oh, what did I say?
Please, tell me, where are you?

Questions

Who are people from your past with whom you would like to reconnect?

What would be the topics that you would discuss over dinner?

STREETS OF CONVERSATION AND FUN

How many conversations do you have each day? What are you trying to do when you talk with people? A person working in retail or real estate will usually say the conversation is about buying and selling. A teacher is likely to say the conversation is about sharing and advising, to assist learning. A doctor will say their conversations are about enquiring, diagnosing and prescribing.

Conversations outside of the work situation take many forms, that cover friendship and banter. Many of the stories in this section reflect the way we often respect each other, in ironic ways, by making fun of each other's activities. For example, 'The Round Object Hunter' tells the tale of two golfers in a friendly battle to see who can win. In contrast, 'Dinki Di And Fair Dinkum' is my view on the type of conversation you could hear in the heat and dust of an Australian country town.

Some of these stories are based on conversations that I have actually had. For example, 'The Dealer' reflects meetings I have had with a friend from Canada. Likewise, the story 'Day At Sea' relates to my memories from a cruise.

All of our conversations are important, as they help us understand people and places. Some conversations have to be serious as they deal with difficult issues. So, some of the stories consider such issues. However, let us have more fun and laughter in our conversations, which I hope these stories will encourage.

Day At Sea

Overview

Cruising has become a preferred holiday for many families and particularly for those who have retired from work.

On ships, which can hold over 5000 people, it is assumed that passengers will have an enjoyable time with few problems. However, that is not always the case, as this story illustrates.

No rush today.
So they say.
Cruising the seaways.
Skipping over the waves.
Time to read, write and drink tea.
To ruminate on poetry.
Such is life at sea.
But, then an emergency.
Heart attack victim.
Into action goes the system.
Roar of thunder over the sea.
Helicopter defying gravity.
Above the noise.
Hold it boys.
Careful, careful!

Push and pull.
Now hoist away.
Okay, okay.
Sail away, sail away.

Question

What is your preferred way of having a holiday?

Dinki Di And Fair Dinkum

Overview

I live in Australia. Originally, there were hundreds of Indigenous languages spoken across this continent. Over the last 200 years, a new version of the English language has emerged. It is called 'Strine'. This story is an imaginary example of it.

Fair Dinkum said to Dinki Di.

'G'day, owsyergoin?'

'All right cobber,' said Dinki Di, 'an' you?'

'Bit crook last week,' said Dinkum, 'but alright now.'

'None of us is gettin' any younger,' said Dinki.

'That's for sure,' said Dinkum.

'Seems like only yesterday, I could work 25 hours a day.'

'And eight days a week,' said Dinki, laughing.

'Takes me all my time to stand still,' said Dinkum, swatting a fly.

Dinki mopped his brow.

'Gee it's 'ot, 'av you got time for a quick one?'

'Sure,' said Dinkum, 'wotel yu av?'

'A schooner of lager, ta.'

'Make it two,' Dinkum said to the barman.

They rested their hats on their chairs and sipped their ale.

'Here's to happiness,' said Dinki, smiling.

'And health and wealth,' said Fair Dinkum, with a grin.

'Do you reckon that 'Rising Star' will win the Cup?'

'My oath, he's a beauty - a racing certainty,' said Dinki.
'Then, here's to a fortune,' said Dinkum, as he raised the betting ticket.
'What about the Wallabies in the World Cup?' enquired Dinki.
'They'll walk it in, standin' on their 'eads,' said Dinkum.
'Another round then,' said Dinki, with a wink.
'Good onya blue,' said Dinkum.
'No worries,' said Dinki Di, 'we'll 'av a great weekend.'
'No bloody worries,' replied Fair Dinkum, 'we've got two winners.'
'Whiskies then,' said Dinkum, in a loud voice.
'Barman, make it a Johnny Wilkinson,' said Dinki.
'Did you mean Johnny Walker?' asked the barman.
'Yeah,' said Dinki.
'I said we'd walk all over 'em didn't I?'
'No bloody worries,' replied Fair Dinkum, 'we've got two winners.'

Question

How is the English language changing, now that it is used in so many different countries?

Don Juan, Peter Pan

Overview

Some people's personalities are larger than life. They live life in the fast lane, with little thought of the bigger picture or their long-term future. Don Juan is an example.

It's a funny kind of world.
For a friend of mine, called Don.
He likes fast cars – like Jaguars.
And lives life on the run.

Oh, he has a way with women
For they like his smile and charm.
But, when they try to tame him
He's nowhere to be found.

Oh, how the ladies like him
With his easy going smile.
It gives him the key to many a door,
Which he opens up in style.

He has a good line in chat shows
Telling stories no one knows.
A raconteur, a *bon viveur*.
That's how the party goes.

Yes, he's a Don Juan, a Peter Pan:
The modern Casanova.
He's here today, but not to stay
When the party's over.

Questions

How would you describe Don Juan, Peter Pan?

Who was the original Casanova, and what did he do in his life to achieve success?

Measuring And Moving

Overview

All of us are going upwards or downwards, and at the same time forwards or backwards. Time waits for no one. All we can do is assess the opportunities and see how many we can seize and develop. So here is a story from the street, of someone who began to think differently about his life.

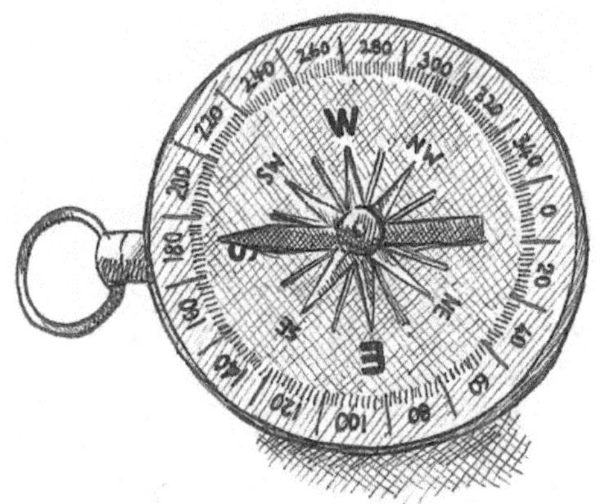

'Which way are you going?' my friend asked.
'What do you mean?' I responded.
'Well you are either going forward or backward.'
'In what way?' I enquired.
'In every way,' he said, as if it was obvious.
Your health is going forward or backwards.
Your relationships are improving or declining.
Your career is flourishing or withering.
Your finances are certainly going up or down.
Nothing stands still,' he summarised.
'Good points,' I said, beginning to feel uncomfortable.
Had I wasted too much of my time?
Procrastinating by putting things off until tomorrow.
What should I have been doing?
'Well, what are you doing to improve things?' he pressed.
I looked at him, as he stood silently waiting for an answer.
'Well I suppose I can try to change a number of things,' I replied.

'My health for instance,' I said.
'Now you're thinking,' he said.
'Yes, everything is moving up or down.'
An image of my bank account balance came into my mind.
I knew that my cash position had been declining for a while.
'Could I cut my costs?
Would I then feel happier?'
Indeed, my measure of personal happiness was going down.
My job had become more of a chore than a challenge.
Fast food and little exercise had taken its toll.
The scales showed my weight was going up
Yet, my speed was going down.
Yes, nothing stood still.
So, I decided I should have up and down measures.
Could I be disciplined and cut my costs?
I planned to increase my walking and running time.
Eating less could also reduce my weight.
How would all this affect my heart rate?
Would it enable me to live longer?
Yes, that was the ultimate measure.
Or was it?
Happiness needed to increase, also.
What is the point of living longer without happiness?
So, more smiles.
More friends.
More enjoyable days.
Yes, my friend was right.
Measuring my actions would help me move forward and upward.
Let the new life begin!

Question

What will you do to measure your own life and move forward?

Next Time Round

Overview

People have different ways of finding their own identity and what is important to them.

This story reflects on a surprising conversation that I had with a retired businessman, whom I had known for a number of years through our mutual interest in golf. But, as this story shows, I did not really know what was important in his life.

'What are you doing in your retirement?' I asked.
'I am Captain of our Golf Club this year,' he replied with a smile.
'It is an honour and my wife and I are invited to many events.'
He picked up his drink of beer and took a sip.
'But, I enjoy gardening and my hobby is ornithology.
Yes, bird watching and long walks keep me active.'
'That is rather different from the life you had in business,' I said.
I knew that he was a well-regarded engineer.
After a long career, he became the CEO of a major company.
'Do you miss the job that you had before retiring?' I asked.
'Not really,' he replied, 'it was full of conflict and stress.'
That is the nature of competition in business.

Lawyers and legal cases replaced old fashioned handshakes.'
He took another drink from his pint of beer.
'If you started again, what kind of work would you do?' I asked.
He put his pint of ale down and laid his hands on the table.
'I would like to be a Franciscan friar,' he said in a quiet way.
Surprised by his reply, I asked him why?
'It fits with who I think I am and would like to be,' he replied.
He paused and I asked him to tell me about the Franciscans.
'Francis of Assisi is said to have started the order in 1208.
He spent a lot of time in prayer and helped the poor.'
'How does a Franciscan friar differ from a monk?' I enquired.
'A friar does not belong to any specific monastery.
He works in the secular world.
There are three main groups.
Friars Minor is an order predominantly for men.
The women's order is called the Poor Clares.
The third group are both men and women and called The Penitents.'
He clearly had researched the history of the three main orders.
'So, if you returned, where would you choose to contribute?'
'Probably the third group, where members can marry', he said.
'I thought Franciscans had to take a vow of chastity,' I enquired.
'A priority is to live a life consistent with the Commandments,' he replied.
'Then, you could do that as part of the Methodists or Baptists,' I noted.
'Maybe, but I am from a Catholic family and education,' he replied.
'We are all conditioned by our experiences,' he explained.
'And your experiences lead you more to the religious life?' I enquired.
'Yes,' he said firmly, 'What is life without faith and belief?'

Questions

What are three important factors in your life?

What action will you take to achieve them?

Running Out Of Time

Overview

Our time is precious and valuable. There are only so many hours in a day and so much to accomplish in that time.

My mother had many sayings that captured my attention. She mentioned the March Hare. Maybe, that is why I am fascinated by people's use of time and the reason I wrote this story.

'I've been running like a March Hare,' she said.
'What do you mean?' I asked.
'So much to do, and not enough time,' she replied.
'That is the problem when you have two jobs.'
'What do you do?' I enquired.
'To earn money for my family, I work in a shop.
Not what I want, but a job is a job.'
'What is the other work that you do?' I asked.
'That is the most important job anyone can have.
But, I don't get any pay for it.'
'What do you mean?' said I, rather puzzled.
'I am a mother of two boys' she said, with a smile.
'So, you work a 16 hour day,' I summarised.
'Yes, seven days a week,' she said, without a smile.
'How do you do it?' I asked.
'With love,' she said, as her smile returned.
'Each morning, I start at six o'clock, to make breakfast.

Then, I take the boys to school and go on the shop.'
'Do you get any time to yourself?' I enquired.
'Very little, as after school I help the boys with their homework.
Also, there is the cleaning and washing and meals to make.'
'You are very busy,' I said.
'Yes, just like the March Hare who runs fast in springtime.
So, I must go, as I am running out of time.'

Questions

What are the priorities in your life that you need to focus upon?

What is your timetable for action in the next month?

The Dealer

Overview

All of life is a negotiation. Every day we are buying and selling. There is a price for everything. We pay in cash or in time.

Those who negotiate the best deals for spending their cash and time, become richer in both money and relationships. Those who negotiate poorly and receive bad deal are usually upset and feel that they have been disadvantaged. This invariably leads to unhappiness. In contrast, those who negotiate well usually feel more powerful and satisfied with the deal.

So, here is a story of someone I met who was street-wise. From the start of every conversation, he considered that he was in a negotiation. He was looking to find out if the other person had something to offer that he wanted and at what price. In return, he perceived he had information and skills to offer, and was trying to see if his contact would buy what he was offering.

To him, the world was one of buyers and sellers engaged in a game of exchange based on negotiation. He would walk into a room and immediately start a conversation on the assumption that the end game was to buy or sell. Negotiation to him was the essence of life. I called him The Dealer. I hope you enjoy his tale, and I wonder how it will influence the way you spend your money and time?

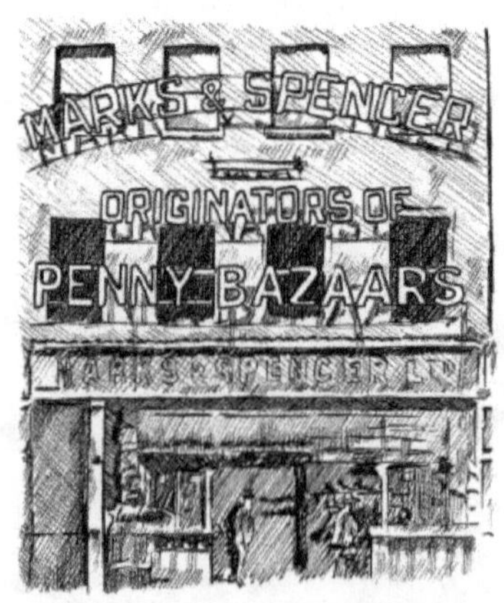

'What's the deal?' he asked smiling, as he shook my hand warmly.
It was the way he always started our discussions.
Most people I knew were more formal.
They would ask, 'How are you?'
Even if they were not concerned about your health.
'Why do you say, what is the deal?' I asked him.
'Well everyone is a buyer or a seller,' he stated.
'I'm usually just gathering information,' I responded.
'So that means you think information is valuable.
And you can use it to improve your ability to buy or sell,' he said quickly.
'At the moment, I am looking for new ideas,' I replied.
'Then you are a potential buyer of ideas.
To improve your education, lifestyle or work?' he enquired with an
engaging laugh.
Already, I could sense the start of the deal.
'Everyone is buying and selling something.
That is the essence of life,' he stated.
'In what way?' I asked, being both sceptical and curious at what I might learn.
'To survive, we all have to give as well as take' he replied.
'Nothing is for free.'
'What about love?' I asked.
'That is one of the biggest deals in the world,' he replied.
'If someone says they love you, they want your time, affection and a
whole lot more.
That is why there are so many prenuptial agreements,' he said with a smile.
'That sounds rather cynical,' I replied.
'Well, look at the ever increasing divorce rate.
There is a price for everything, but it is not always paid in money,' he replied.
'Do you mean mutual favours?' I asked
'Yes, so many deals are done on the basis of I will help you if you will
help me.'
'Yes, but a lot of people do favours without expecting a reward,'
I said - recognising part of my own pattern of behaviour.
'That means they have a debt of time to the other person.
It is called social exchange, or a deal by another name,' he said.
'The more you want something or someone, the higher the price.'
'The Law of Supply and Demand,' I said.
'It is the basis of all deals,' he said.
'What happens if people do not recognise they are perceived as
valuable?' I asked.

'They will be exploited,' he said.
'The deal always reflects the perception of value.
That is why lawyers and accountants restrict the numbers who enter their professions.'
'So, what about families?' I asked.
'Relationships between family members are not based on deals,' I said.
'That is where most real deals are done,' he replied.
'Family members help each other on the expectation others will help them.
Particularly in their old age,' he added, ruefully.
'To me, a deal is more associated with business,' I said.
'Yes, business revolves around deals,' he replied.
'The deals determine who wins and who loses.
If you price too low you will suffer.
If you price too high you can fail.
Doing the right deal at the right price is easy to say but hard to do.'
'So, it is all about judgement,' I said.
'For sure,' he replied smiling.
'There are no guarantees in this world.
You are as only as good as the deals you make.
I need to find a deal,' he said.
'There are none here,' and he smiled and walked away.

Questions

To what extent are you a good negotiator, and in what ways?

What have you learned from this story that can help you on your journey through life?

The Round Object Hunter

Overview

Sport is increasingly dominated by money and lawyers, as television contracts provide substantial income for the best players. This is particularly so in the game of golf, where many professionals are multi-millionaires. At the local club level, there is still a high level of competitiveness in the various competitions. The prize may only be the pleasure of winning, but pride is also at stake.

This story reflects the way the game of golf can be both a competitive drama, and a comedy, at the same time.

Stalking the area, like the hunter of old, he moved towards his target.
He entered the thick undergrowth, fearless of the risks involved.
Moving meticulously, his eyes were glued to the ground.
The sharp crack of a twig, like the sound of a gun, did not disturb him.
Nor did the dense foliage, previously undisturbed by human hand.
This was jungle country, the land of the intrepid explorer.

Silence, interrupted only by the odd curse and oath, marked the search.
Armed only with a club, looking for clues, no thought for personal safety.
'We've only got two minutes left,' he said, as another hunter arrived.
Desperation showed, as they flayed the ground.
And then a find, deep in the bushes.
Excitedly, he plucked the white object from its lair.
'Unplayable lie, drop for one,' he said, just as he saw a GUR sign.
'Ground Under Repair, it's a free drop,' he said with a smile.

'So it is,' said his partner, 'but is that your ball?'
The hunter looked at the unusual and unknown mark.
Letting out a mighty oath, he swung his arm over.
The offending object disappeared deep into the jungle.
'Stroke and distance penalty for lost ball?'
'And three off the tee,' said his partner, trying to keep a straight face.
'What, and let that four ball behind play through?' said the hunter.
'Not bloody likely! You're one up.'
'Let's go to the Pond Hole and see if you can do some fishing.'

Question

What are the main sports that you play, and what have you learned about yourself from doing so?

Your Future

Overview

Some people take out insurance. Others say their prayers. Doctors advise that regular exercise is beneficial. Psychologists say that we need to have an optimistic and positive mind-set. There are no guarantees about our future, although this story may be of help.

'How do you see the future?' he asked.
'About what?' I replied.
'Whatever future you have in mind,' he answered.
Seeking clarification, I enquired.
'Are you asking about my work or health?'
'They are related to each other,' he replied with a smile.
'If you are unhappy at work, it will affect your health.'
'Yes,' I said, 'I have experienced that.'
'So, how did you deal with it?' he asked sympathetically.
'After looking at other options, I took another job.'
'So, you imagined a new future that would be better?'
'It was a risk, but I felt it worthwhile,' I replied.
'Nothing is ever perfect, but it was better than the previous job.'
'And how do you see the future now?' he asked.
'Things are going well, so I am content,' I said.
'That is dangerous,' he countered with a worried look.
'Why should that be so?' I enquired, in a perplexed way.
'Because you are likely to take things too easy,' he replied.
'If so, you will give up thinking about the future.'

Deep down, I suspected he was right.
I had been taking things for granted.
Instead of planning for the future, I was reacting to events.
'What do you think are the things that could upset your life?' he asked.
'Health is the one thing I can't control,' I replied.
'Well you can reduce risks,' he said.
'Eat well, exercise and have positive thoughts,' he added.
'They can help determine your future.'
It was sound advice.
But, always harder to do than say.
'What about your relationships?' he asked.
'Do you have the people in your life that you want?'
This was now becoming more personal.
'There are some people who annoy me,' I said, trying to be vague.
'Your future will depend on the people around you.
The older you get, the more you need support,' he advised.
Feeling my bones creak more each day, I smiled.
'Don't rely on family and friends,' he warned.
'Why not?' I asked, as I had a lot of both.
'Age will also attack them, perhaps quicker than it hits you.'
I realised he could be right, as many family and friends were not well.
'Prepare to pay for help in all kinds of ways,' he continued.
'Yes, money talks when you are old,' he concluded.
I began to count my savings.
Did I have enough?
'You will need strangers, as well as family and friends.
'They will help you, if you help them earn enough to pay their bills.'
Suddenly, I could see what he meant about not being too content.
His question about how I saw the future was rather scary.
I shook his hand and said I was off to manage my future.

Questions

What are you doing to prepare for your future, in terms of your training and development?

What are your plans for the next five to ten years?

Roads Of Life

Overview

We all have choices to make in life. Some are forced upon us by circumstances. However, we are taught that if we develop our knowledge and skills, we will have more options. Therefore, we look for careers that give us satisfaction. We look for relationships that will make us happier. We decide to live in places that we feel will provide a community of support.

In making our choices, we are travelling down various roads of life. These roads will give us experiences and involve decisions that will determine how satisfied we are. This story reflects key questions that we can consider. How will you decide which road to take in the next phase of your life?

I came to a roundabout
An old man was there, resting on a stick.
'What is the best road to take?' I asked.
'It depends on what you want in life', he replied.
'What choices do I have?' I enquired.
He answered, 'straight ahead is the road to Opportunity.
It is uphill, hard to climb and requires creativity.
The places on the way are called Risk and Optimism.

To the right is the road to Hope.
It is a tough and rough pathway.
You will need strong beliefs and determination.
Places *en route* are called Imagination and Perseverance
To the left is the road to Glory.
You will see battlefields on your way.
No Man's Land stands between Defeat and Victory.
Monuments can be seen at a place called Memorial.'
'Let me think about the choices', I said.
'What if I do not like any of the roads?'.
'Returning down the road from whence you came is an option.
It is called the road of Repetition.
You will pass places called Regrets and Mistakes.
They will look familiar.
But, it is all an illusion.
Nothing stays the same.
You can move backwards or forwards.
In so doing, you will go mentally upwards or downwards,' he
replied.
'All the options you have given are uncertain,' I said.
'Yes,' replied the old man, 'there is no road to Certainty.
Life would be boring if that was the case.
All you can do is to aim for success.'
'How do I do that?' I asked.
'Plan for the worst and don't give up' he said.
'Train hard and be positive.
Your attitude to failure will determine how far you go.
Remember success is a state of mind, not a destination.
It is all a matter of perception.
Now, which road will you take?'

Questions

What are the main roads in life that you have taken so far?

Which roads do you plan to take in the future?

About the Author

Dr Charles Margerison is a Psychologist and a member of the Royal Institution and the Royal Society of Literature. He is a member of the Association for the Teaching of Psychology. He is also Chairman of Viewpoint Resources Ltd, a publishing organisation, and the founder and President of Amazing People Worldwide® and The Amazing People Institute. He was a co-founder of Emerald Insights, the management journal publishing company. Previously, he was Professor of Management at the University of Cranfield, UK, and also at the University of Queensland, Australia. He is the co-founder of Team Management Systems.

The author of many books on management and education issues, Dr Margerison has also written an innovative continuing professional development system, called *The Communication and Problem Solving Resource*. This provides continued professional development training and support resources for use in schools, colleges and business organisations.

The Amazing People Worldwide® Series commenced when Dr Margerison wondered what people like William Shakespeare, Marie Curie, Abraham Lincoln, and other great achievers would have said if he had interviewed them about their life and work. He decided to research the known facts about their lives and write up what he thought they would say. In particular, he focused on the psychological issues associated with their personalities, and how they used their time and talents well in order to achieve. The stories give us an insight into their motivation and relationships with other people. The publications include *Amazing Careers, Amazing Women, Amazing Scientists, Amazing Musicians, Amazing Entrepreneurs* and many more.

This unique collection of stories is presented via a new concept called BioViews that combines biography with a virtual interview. The stories are an interpretation of the life stories of amazing people. Each one is presented as if the person is talking to you personally.

BioViews offer new and interesting ways of understanding major contributions made to our world by amazing people. The stories are inspirational and we hope they can help you achieve your own ambitions in your own journey through life.

To facilitate student participation, Dr Margerison has also written a variety of music education resources, and a collection of children's interactive stories for young children, including the *Imagineland* series, and the *Can Do Kids* world travel series. Most recently, the organisation has launched a whole school resource suite focussed on supporting character education and wellbeing through the power of positive psychology and story-telling called *Amazing People Schools*. This website is packed with teacher and student resources that help students develop their self-understanding and encourage them to be the best that they can be, and is used in schools to support Character Education and Wellbeing.

Acknowledgements

My personal thanks to Monica Lawlor, Frances Corcoran, Catherine Hodgkinson and Marion Andersson, for their continued support, encouragement, ideas and great co-ordination and editing skills.

The majority of the images which accompany my poems are drawn by Emily Hamilton. The remainder of the images are from the websites Public Domain Vectors, SVG Silh, Needpix or Cliparts 101, copyright free repositories.